Strategies for Common Core Mathematics

Implementing the Standards for Mathematical Practice, K–5

Leslie A. Texas and Tammy L. Jones

Eye On Education
6 Depot Way West, Suite 106
Larchmont, NY 10538
(914) 833-0551
(914) 833-0761 fax
www.eyeoneducation.com

Library of Congress Cataloging-in-Publication Data

Texas, Leslie A.
Strategies for common core mathematics. Implementing the standards for mathematical
practice, K–5/Leslie A. Texas and Tammy L. Jones.
     pages   cm
ISBN 978-1-59667-242-0
1. Mathematics—Study and teaching (Elementary)
2. Mathematics—Study and teaching (Elementary)—Standards—United States.
I. Jones, Tammy L.
II. Title.
QA135.6.J663 2013
372.702′1873—dc23   2013001369

10 9 8 7 6 5 4 3 2 1

Sponsoring Editor: Robert Sickles
Production Editors: Lauren Beebe and Lauren Davis
Copyeditor: Laurie Lieb
Designer and Compositor: Matthew Williams, click! Publishing Services
Cover Designer: Armen Kojoyian

Acknowledgments

We would first like to thank Eye On Education for the opportunity to develop this series of books. A special thank you to Bob Sickles, President of Eye On Education, for his continued support and patience throughout this project. To the editorial staff, thank you for your excellent guidance and expeditious feedback. We would also like to express gratitude to the many students, teachers, schools, and districts with which we have worked over the years. You have allowed us the opportunity to develop, use, and refine these strategies in classrooms across the country. Finally, thanks to our families for their support and encouragement while on this journey.

Meet the Authors

Leslie A. Texas has over twenty years of experience working with K–12 teachers and schools across the country to enhance rigorous and relevant instruction. She believes that improving student outcomes depends on comprehensive approaches to teaching and learning. She taught middle- and high-school mathematics and science, and has strong content expertise in both areas. Through her advanced degree studies, she honed her skills in content and program development and student-centered instruction. Using a combination of direct instruction, modeling, and problem-solving activities rooted in practical application of mathematical principles, Leslie helps teachers become more effective classroom leaders and peer coaches.

An educator since 1979, **Tammy L. Jones** has worked with students from first grade through college. Currently, Tammy is consulting with individual school districts in training mathematics teachers on effective techniques for being successful in the mathematics classroom. As a classroom teacher Tammy's goal was that all students understand and appreciate the mathematics they were studying; that they could read it, write it, explore it, and communicate it with confidence; and that they would be able to use mathematics as they need to in their lives. She believes that problem solving, followed by a well-reasoned presentation of results, is central to the process of learning mathematics, and that this learning happens most effectively in a cooperative, student-centered classroom. Tammy believes that mathematics is experiential and in her current consulting work creates and shares mathematical experiences.

A lifelong learner, Tammy is an active member in the National Council of Teachers of Mathematics and its Tennessee affiliates as well as a T^3 Instructor for Texas Instruments. Serving on the Mathematics Feedback Group for the Common Core Standards gave Tammy a unique perspective on the development of the Standards and allowed special insight into the development of this series.

Supplemental Downloads

Several of the figures discussed and displayed in this book are also available on Eye On Education's website as Adobe Acrobat files. Permission has been granted to purchasers of this book to download these resources and print them.

You can access the downloads by visiting www.eyeoneducation.com. From the home page, click on the "Free" tab, and then click on "Supplemental Downloads." Alternatively, you can search or browse our website for this book's product page, and click on "Log in to Access Supplemental Downloads."

Your book-buyer access code is **SCC-7242-0**.

Index of Supplemental Downloads

Five-Step Problem-Solving Process Graphic Organizers 103
Visual Vocabulary Concept-Mapping Template 105
ABC Sum Race Scorecards 117
Grid Games Scorecards 124
Matching Mania Scorecards 130
What's My Move? Game Boards 148

Contents

Foreword ix

Preface: A Note to Our Readers xi

Section 1: The Doorway to the Common Core 1
The Common Core State Standards for Mathematics 2
The Standards for Mathematical Practice 2
The Standards for Mathematical Practice versus the Content Standards 4
How the Standards for Mathematical Practice Support
    the Content Standards 4
Teaching the Standards for Mathematical Practice 5
The Doorway to the Standards for Mathematical Practice 5
Strategies Matrix 8

Section 2: Framing Strategies for Implementing SMPs #1, #5, and #6 ... 9
    The Strategies 13
Problem-Solving Process 15
    Overview 15
    Directions 16
    Common Core State Standards for Mathematics Addressed 18
    Primary Example 19
    Guided Facilitation 20
    Elementary Example 23
    Guided Facilitation 23
Visual Vocabulary 27
    Overview 27
    Directions 27
    Common Core State Standards for Mathematics Addressed 27
    Examples 28
    Guided Facilitation 29
Puzzling Problems 33
    Overview 33
    Directions 33
    Common Core State Standards for Mathematics Addressed 34
    Primary Example 36
    Grades 2–3 Example 37
    Grades 4–5 Example 38
    Guided Facilitation 39

Section 3: Strategies for Implementing Combinations of SMPs 41
    The Strategies 45

ABC Sum Race...47
    Overview...47
    Directions...47
    Common Core State Standards for Mathematics Addressed.........47
    Examples...50
    Guided Facilitation...52
Grid Games...53
    Overview...53
    Directions...53
    Common Core State Standards for Mathematics Addressed.........54
    Example: What's My Shape?...56
    Example: Perimeter and Area...56
    Guided Facilitation...57
Matching Mania...59
    Overview...59
    Directions...59
    Common Core State Standards for Mathematics Addressed.........60
    Example: One-Digit Operations...62
    Example: Factors and Primes...66
    Example: Operations with Fractions 2...70
    Guided Facilitation...77
Walk This Way...79
    Overview...79
    Directions...79
    Common Core State Standards for Mathematics Addressed.........80
What's My Move?...85
    Overview...85
    Directions...85
    Common Core State Standards for Mathematics Addressed.........85
    Primary Example...89
    Guided Facilitation...89
    Elementary Example...95
    Guided Facilitation...95

Appendix A: Blackline Masters for Strategies and Illustrations............103
    Five-Step Problem-Solving Process Graphic Organizers 103
    Visual Vocabulary Concept-Mapping Template.......................105
    Puzzling Problems Tasks, Answer Keys...106
    ABC Sum Race Sample Cards, Scorecards, Answer Key 117
    Grid Games Tasks, Scorecards, Answer Keys.......................124
    Matching Mania Tasks, Scorecards, Answer Keys.....................130
    What's My Move? Game Boards...148

Appendix B: Common Core State Standards for Mathematics Resources...153
    Standards for Mathematical Practice...153
    CCSSM K–5 Nomenclature Key...158
    Standards Alignment—Primary...159
    Standards Alignment—Elementary...161

References 163

Foreword

Will Rogers is credited with saying, "When you are dissatisfied and unhappy with your adult life and think you would like to return to your youth, you will feel better if you remember you would have to take Algebra." Although said in jest, many adults remember the frustrations and lack of success they experienced in mathematics. In spite of increased efforts to improve the teaching of mathematics in the past two decades, Algebra 1 remains one of the highest failing courses in U.S. schools. For current students, the rigor proposed in the Common Core mathematics standards adds to their fears and frustrations. Teachers and school administrators will find the three books written by Leslie A. Texas and Tammy L. Jones helpful in preparing students, beginning in kindergarten, to think mathematically and come to enjoy participating in such thinking. In a unique way, these talented authors provide:

- Strategies for engaging students in mathematical discussions
- Strategies that allow for differentiation—both individually and in small groups
- Strategies that involve cooperative learning environments and small-group problem solving
- Strategies that can be tools for diagnosing student misconceptions and then making modifications for individual student needs; for example, some of the books' Guided Facilitation sections identify common student misconceptions and ideas for addressing them
- Questioning strategies that allow students to arrive at the "ah-ha" moment when investigating a topic so they can create their own understanding upon which later topics will be built. This practice is a critical shift in what traditionally has been the delivery of mathematics instruction. This concept of teaching is critical throughout the grade levels if we ever expect to address the high failure rates in Algebra I.

Collectively, Texas and Jones have 40 years of classroom experience teaching mathematics in elementary, middle, and high schools, which include teaching in urban, suburban, rural, and private school settings. Being active members of their professional organizations, such as the National Council of Teachers of Mathematics (NCTM), has allowed them to model lifelong learning for both their students and their peers.

In addition to their classroom teaching, these skilled authors have provided professional development for teachers and students from kindergarten through college level in 40 states. Their work has included helping develop standards and curriculum at the state level as well as implementing curriculum and best-practice strategies at the classroom level. One of the characteristics that places Texas and Jones in heavy demand as consultants is their ability to model and offer teachers support throughout the school year, a practice that builds capacity at both building and district levels. As a result of the authors' consulting experiences, all of the strategies contained in this series have been implemented successfully in multiple classrooms around the country.

Educators who have the responsibility of teaching mathematics will find the strategies provided in these three books to be critical tools in improving the mathematical skills of students in grades K–12. If implemented with fidelity, eventually Will Rogers can be proven wrong by increasing the number of adults who reflect on their youth and think of Algebra as a positive experience! (Or think of Algebra positively!)

Robert Lynn Canady, Professor Emeritus
University of Virginia, Charlottesville, VA

Preface:
A Note to Our Readers

When we took on the task of writing this book, we asked ourselves two questions: So What? and Who Cares? Why write a book about the mathematical practices and how could we do it in such a way that would make a difference? These were certainly the questions that guided our process as we developed the materials contained within these pages. Practical, versatile, easy to implement, promotes student engagement, yields results—these were the criteria we used as a guideline for selecting the strategies for this book. Other questions we thought might be of interest as well as our responses are listed below:

Why are the same strategies used in all three books in the series?

We intentionally chose strategies versatile enough to be used across the grade levels so we could illustrate the progression of concept development designed in the Common Core State Standards for Mathematics. Explicitly illustrating the scaffolding of skills across the levels emphasizes the importance of developing the mathematical practices at each level to ensure success as students transition to the next level.

How can I teach all my content standards using the strategies in this book?

All the strategies contained in this book are versatile and can be used with any content standards you choose. We have included content-specific examples to illustrate how the strategy works, but none of the strategies are limited to the mathematical concepts shown.

How do I know these strategies will work in my classroom?

These are proven strategies that have been implemented in our own classrooms as well as in hundreds of classrooms around the country. They were intentionally chosen based on their ease of use and the impact they have had on student engagement and achievement. Some of the strategies were shared by teachers with whom we work; permission for their use has been given.

How can I develop mathematical thinkers *and* provide an opportunity for computational proficiency?

The Common Core requires that students be able to engage in mathematical discourse using their understanding and knowledge of the mathematical content. In order to gain mastery, they need to practice the skills. This means working math problems in order to become computationally proficient. So how can you take a basic problem set and make it into a rich and engaging task? This book contains specific strategies that illustrate how to engage students in computational practice; other strategies promote higher-order thinking and in-depth problem solving.

Why would I buy this book when there is so much free stuff out there?

There are many fantastic resources available on the Internet. For example, the sites containing assessment tasks addressing the critical content and skills of the Common Core State Standards are tremendously valuable. The value of this book is that it not only contains strategies to prepare students for these rigorous assessments, but also provides practical notes on how to implement them effectively. You can even take the released items from the websites and use them as the content for the strategies shared in the book.

The Doorway to the Common Core

The Common Core State Standards for Mathematics

With the creation of the Common Core State Standards for Mathematics (CCSSM), a new era in mathematics education began for those states that adopted them. States that have adopted the CCSSM now have a common goal in mathematics education.

> Building on the excellent foundation of standards states have laid, the Common Core State Standards are the first step in providing our young people with a high-quality education. It should be clear to every student, parent, and teacher what the standards of success are in every school. (Common Core State Standards Initiative, 2012a)

How clear is it "what the standards of success are"? The standards were written "to provide a clear and consistent framework to prepare our children for college and the workforce" (Common Core State Standards Initiative, 2012a).

In its *Myths vs Facts* section, the CORE Standards website (www.corestandards.org/about-the-standards/myths-vs-facts) states that the standards "are not a curriculum. They are a clear set of shared goals and expectations for what knowledge and skills will help our students succeed." What are the implications for the classroom teacher, whether teaching kindergarten or high-school algebra? Teachers need to become fluent in the content not only to teach their grade and course, but also to reinforce the prior content knowledge of their students and understand how the current content supports where the students are going. Only through studying these progressions will teachers truly be able to connect the mathematics they are teaching to what their students have previously learned and to what will be expected of them in upcoming grades.

The Standards for Mathematical Practice

According to the Common Core State Standards for Mathematics, "The Standards for Mathematical Practice describe varieties of expertise that mathematics educators at all levels should seek to develop in their students" (2012b). The National Council of Teachers of Mathematics (NCTM), in its *Principles and Standards for School Mathematics (PSSM)*, states that "the five Process Standards highlight ways of acquiring and applying content knowledge" (2005, p. 29).

The Standards for Mathematical Practice (SMP) are based upon the NCTM process standards and the strands of mathematical proficiency in the National Research Council's report *Adding It Up*. NCTM chose to present its mathematical processes from the point of view that these are a collection of best practices that teachers can utilize to help their students develop a depth of understanding of key mathematical concepts that also leads to increased retention of those concepts.

Here are the eight Standards for Mathematical Practice (Common Core State Standards Initiative, 2012b):

1. Make sense of problems and persevere in solving them.
2. Reason abstractly and quantitatively.
3. Construct viable arguments and critique the reasoning of others.
4. Model with mathematics.
5. Use appropriate tools strategically.
6. Attend to precision.
7. Look for and make use of structure.
8. Look for and express regularity in repeated reasoning.

The content standards provide the context, whereas the Standards for Mathematical Practice assist students in developing mathematical proficiency. The eight practices are distinct from one another but interconnected in ways that support students in becoming mathematically proficient. Expertise is generated in practice but implemented through process.

> **Expertise is generated in practice but implemented through process.**

These practices need to be incorporated into daily classroom instruction. The creators of the Common Core State Standards for Mathematics took the perspective that the Standards for Mathematical Practice are observable indicators of student understanding that identify the level of expertise that teachers should foster in their students. The writers for the CCSSM even argue that a lack of understanding in the mathematical content inhibits students from participating in the mathematical practices. But it is the practices themselves that help develop that understanding. So connecting the content to the mathematical practices is critical if teachers want to develop solid mathematical proficiency in their students (Common Core State Standards Initiative, 2012b).

Will these mathematical practices look the same in a kindergarten classroom as in a high-school mathematics classroom? Not necessarily. The students are at a different level in their journey toward attaining expertise in various mathematical topics and skills. Students need procedural fluency in a topic as well as an understanding of the concept. **It is for this reason there are three books in this series so these differences can be addressed specifically for each grade band.**

The processes are how a student gains proficiencies in the content that allows them to develop the practices that ultimately carry them through their mathematical journey. The CCSSM are a collection of processes, proficiencies, and practices that produces students who are ready for successful transition into the workplace or college.

The Standards for Mathematical Practice versus the Content Standards

The Standards for Mathematical Practice identify the habits that mathematically proficient students have developed. Habits are developed over time. How long it takes to develop a habit is debatable. But clearly, mathematically proficient students, those who have developed these eight habits, have experienced mathematics regularly and consistently over a period of time.

> The processes are how students gain proficiencies in the content that allow them to develop the practices that ultimately become sound habits.

The Standards for Mathematical Practice are how the student engages with the mathematical content to develop both procedural fluency and conceptual understanding. They are separate, yet must be developed together to ensure that students can effectively understand the content and engage in the practices. The processes are how students gain proficiencies in the content that allow them to develop the practices that ultimately become sound habits.

How the Standards for Mathematical Practice Support the Content Standards

For students to connect the practices to the content, teachers need to understand how students learn mathematics and that not all students learn the same way or in the same time frame. Teachers will need to provide opportunities for students to delve deeply into a concept by designing lessons that explicitly embed and utilize the Standards for Mathematical Practice.

The eight Standards for Mathematical Practice are not experienced in isolation. In fact, most of the time, students simultaneously employ several of the practices as they engage in mathematical experiences. If students are to "construct viable arguments and critique the reasoning of others," they will need to "attend to precision" by using precise vocabulary and symbolism. They will then check the reasonableness of their solutions by gathering supporting evidence. Students who "look for and make use of structure" will also "look for and express regularity in repeated reasoning" while they "make sense of problems and persevere in solving them." Along the way they also "use appropriate tools strategically."

The content standards also support the practices. The writers identify "potential 'points of intersection'" between the content and the SMP as places where the content mastery requires a level of deeper understanding.

The Partnership for Assessment of Readiness for College and Careers (PARCC) Content Framework for Mathematics notes that "opportunities for in-depth work on key concepts and connections to critical practices . . . intend to support . . . efforts to deliver instruction that connects content and practices while achieving the standards' balance of conceptual understanding, procedural skill and fluency, and application" (n.d., para. 3).

Teaching the Standards for Mathematical Practice

Teaching students to become mathematical thinkers does not happen randomly. In order for students to meet the expectations of high-level content knowledge contained in the CCSSM, it is necessary for the students to build a foundation of thinking and communicating mathematically. These practices, outlined in the Standards for Mathematical Practice, must be explicitly and intentionally designed into the curriculum and become a focus of instructional practice in the classroom.

The next section contains strategies for teaching the mathematical practices while simultaneously addressing the content of the Common Core State Standards for Mathematics. These ideas were chosen for their flexibility: they can be taught at any grade level and address almost any concept. In addition, they are easy to prepare and implement. This allows for continued use and refinement while, at the same time, not requiring an added burden of hours of preparation. The section contains an overall description as well as detailed directions for implementation of each strategy. See the Strategies Matrix (page 8) for an overview of mapping each strategy to the SMP.

The Doorway to the Standards for Mathematical Practice

The Standards for Mathematical Practice can be seen as the doorway to implementing the Common Core State Standards for Mathematics. Students, as well as educators and administrators, need to understand what these eight practices entail and what they might look like in their classrooms and mathematical experiences. These standards can be grouped into various clusters to represent differing foci. For the purpose of developing strategies to support the implementation of the CCSSM, the SMP can be grouped as shown in the doorway graphic (page 6).

A door provides the first impression of what lies beyond. When the door is open, it invites one to enter and experience what is behind it. When a door is closed, it evokes a sense of mystery and the unknown. For some educators, the SMP are an open door to the CCSSM. These educators are familiar with implementing process standards through research-based strategies and guiding their students to a deeper understanding of mathematical concepts. For others, the SMP are viewed as a locked door through which they have yet to enter. They have guided their students to a library

Standards for
Mathematical Practice

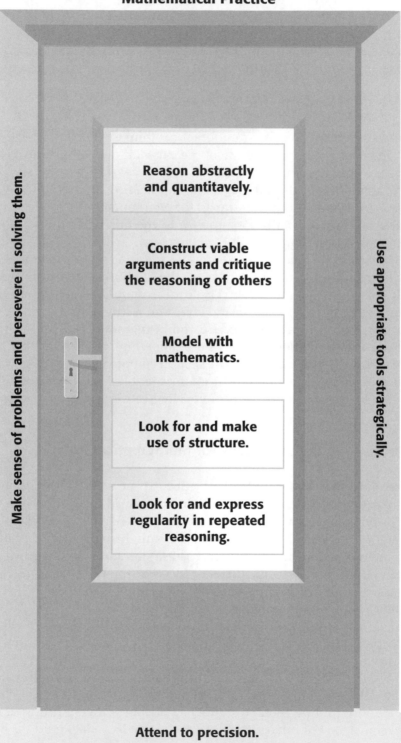

Make sense of problems and persevere in solving them.

Use appropriate tools strategically.

Reason abstractly and quantitavely.

Construct viable arguments and critique the reasoning of others

Model with mathematics.

Look for and make use of structure.

Look for and express regularity in repeated reasoning.

Attend to precision.

filled with procedural worksheets and surface-skimming algorithmic mathematics.

A door cannot function without a frame. The frame is the support system that holds the door in place. The two SMP that serve as the frame of the door are the following:

1. Make sense of problems and persevere in solving them.
5. Use appropriate tools strategically.

The threshold is another integral part of a door. The function of the threshold is to provide a transition between the inside and the outside or between rooms. SMP #6 "**Attend to precision,**" serves as the threshold for the SMP doorway to the CCSSM. It is through precise and effective communication that students are able to gain insights about how they think about mathematics. As NCTM states in *PSSM*, "It is important to give students experiences that help them appreciate the power and precision of mathematical language" (2005, p. 63).

If a door is locked, keys are required to gain entry. Being the guardian of the keys was historically a very high honor and came with great responsibility. The key to unlocking the door of the SMP is being deliberate and intentional in their implementation. It is one thing to say the SMP are embedded in daily instruction. It is another to actually seamlessly interweave the mathematical practices with content instruction. The following strategies will aid in unlocking, opening, and successfully going through the doorway of the Standards for Mathematical Practice to implement the CCSSM effectively.

Strategies Matrix

Strategies		SMP #1 Make sense of problems and persevere in solving them.	SMP #2 Reason abstractly and quantitatively.	SMP #3 Construct viable arguments and critique the reasoning of others.	SMP #4 Model with mathematics.	SMP #5 Use appropriate tools strategically.	SMP #6 Attend to precision.	SMP #7 Look for and make use of structure.	SMP #8 Look for and express regularity in repeated reasoning.
Framing Strategies	Problem-Solving Process	✓	✓	✓	✓	✓		✓	✓
	Visual Vocabulary	✓	✓	✓	✓	✓	✓	✓	✓
	Puzzling Problems	✓	✓	✓	✓	✓	✓	✓	✓
Strategies	ABC Sum Race	✓		✓		✓	✓		
	Grid Games	✓	✓	✓	✓	✓	✓	✓	✓
	Matching Mania	✓	✓	✓	✓	✓	✓	✓	✓
	Walk This Way	✓			✓	✓	✓		✓
	What's My Move?	✓	✓	✓		✓	✓	✓	✓

---■---

Framing Strategies for Implementing SMPs #1, #5, and #6

The following three Standards for Mathematical Practice, SMP #1, SMP #5, and SMP #6, serve as the frame for the door and the threshold for the door. Students who venture through this door are on a journey that promotes processes, proficiencies, and practices in the Common Core mathematics classroom. These three practices are pivotal, not only because they develop conceptual understanding of the content, but also because they play an integral role in the implementation of the other five practices. These practices should permeate the mathematics classroom environment and become part of the daily fabric of both mathematics instruction and the students' mathematics experience.

1. Make sense of problems and persevere in solving them.
Mathematically proficient students start by explaining to themselves the meaning of a problem and looking for entry points to its solution. They analyze givens, constraints, relationships, and goals. They make conjectures about the form and meaning of the solution and plan a solution pathway rather than simply jumping into a solution attempt. They consider analogous problems, and try special cases and simpler forms of the original problem in order to gain insight into its solution. They monitor and evaluate their progress and change course if necessary. Older students might, depending on the context of the problem, transform algebraic expressions or change the viewing window on their graphing calculator to get the information they need. Mathematically proficient students can explain correspondences between equations, verbal descriptions, tables, and graphs or draw diagrams of important features and relationships, graph data, and search for regularity or trends. Younger students might rely on using concrete objects or pictures to help conceptualize and solve a problem. Mathematically proficient students check their answers to problems using a different method, and they continually ask themselves, "Does this make sense?" They can understand the approaches of others to solving complex problems and identify correspondences between different approaches. (Common Core State Standards Initiative, 2012b)

As children move into their elementary years, they begin to understand the need for more efficient strategies as the knowledge they are acquiring extends to fractions and decimal fractions. They see how problem solving makes use of the structures of mathematics. An example of this structure can be seen when children understand how inverse operations aid in the investigation of problems. Students begin to more fully develop metacognition in a mathematics classroom where reflection, estimation, and checking for the reasonableness of an answer are the norm. Problems can be posed that are more complex and require a greater cognitive demand.

Students will still look for a place to enter the problem and apply a strategy, then analyze to see if it is going to work or if they need to back up and start again.

5. Use appropriate tools strategically.

Mathematically proficient students consider the available tools when solving a mathematical problem. These tools might include pencil and paper, concrete models, a ruler, a protractor, a calculator, a spreadsheet, a computer algebra system, a statistical package, or dynamic geometry software. Proficient students are sufficiently familiar with tools appropriate for their grade or course to make sound decisions about when each of these tools might be helpful, recognizing both the insight to be gained and their limitations. For example, mathematically proficient high school students analyze graphs of functions and solutions generated using a graphing calculator. They detect possible errors by strategically using estimation and other mathematical knowledge. When making mathematical models, they know that technology can enable them to visualize the results of varying assumptions, explore consequences, and compare predictions with data. Mathematically proficient students at various grade levels are able to identify relevant external mathematical resources, such as digital content located on a website, and use them to pose or solve problems. They are able to use technological tools to explore and deepen their understanding of concepts. (Common Core State Standards Initiative, 2012b)

A tool is some type of device that allows a person to carry out a particular function. There are many tools that can be used in a primary mathematics classroom. Everything from paper and pencil to manipulatives to various forms of technology, including calculators and dynamic computer software, can be thought of as a tool. These become tools of investigation for students as they are doing mathematics. Students need to experience mathematics, and the use of tools of investigation allows them that experience. Elementary students add appropriate tools to their primary toolbox, which contains the various tools that were available to them in K–2. The use of ten frames and base-ten materials in primary grades is now extended to a more strategic use of the base-ten materials as a strategy for modeling and working with place value. Students understand how to use these new tools effectively and know when and why it is more efficient and strategic to use each tool. Students need to know and understand the benefits as well as the limitations of various tools. They need to recognize that tools are a way to explore and deepen their understanding of various concepts. Students also need to be able to use estimation to check for the reasonableness of an answer.

6. Attend to precision.

Mathematically proficient students try to communicate precisely to others. They try to use clear definitions in discussion with others and in their own reasoning. They state the meaning of the symbols they choose, including using the equal sign consistently and appropriately. They are careful about specifying units of measure, and labeling axes to clarify the correspondence with quantities in a problem. They calculate accurately and efficiently, express numerical answers with a degree of precision appropriate for the problem context. In the elementary grades, students give carefully formulated explanations to each other. By the time they reach high school they have learned to examine claims and make explicit use of definitions. (Common Core State Standards Initiative, 2012b)

NCTM considers communication

a way of sharing ideas and clarifying understanding. Through communication, ideas become objects of reflection, refinement, discussion, and amendment. The communication process also helps build meaning and permanence for ideas and makes them public. When students are challenged to think and reason about mathematics and to communicate the results of their thinking to others orally or in writing, they learn to be clear and convincing. (NCTM, 2005, p. 60)

Communication can be oral or written: it can employ a visual model or graphic. Students should not memorize a definition just to spit it out again. The purpose of learning vocabulary is to use it later to facilitate building the structures of mathematics. Vocabulary in any discipline usually has connotations specific for that discipline. That is one of the challenges in a technical subject such as mathematics. However, the teacher is the person responsible for monitoring students' precise use of vocabulary, units of measure, symbols, and other mathematical language.

Students who are mathematically proficient and use clear and concise vocabulary, symbol notation, and units are the students who gain deeper insights into the mathematics they are studying. Elementary students need to discuss and communicate with drawings and concrete models. They need to be encouraged to continue to write about mathematics. Oral discussions, concrete models, and drawings need to build naturally to writing about their investigations and reasoning. As children practice and continue on their journey through mathematics, they will develop better communication skills and more formal approaches to their writing and justifications, if guided. Students will begin to use more mathematically precise language as they critique their peers' work and engage in discussions. The simple familiar language used in early grades begins to give way to the more formal language of mathematics in elementary grades.

The Strategies

The following three strategies illustrate how these three practices permeate the other five.

- ◆ **Problem-Solving Process** offers a graphic organizer and an approach for solving problems that can make contextual problem solving accessible to diverse students.
- ◆ **Visual Vocabulary** offers strategies for students to go beyond rote memorization of words to developing true understanding of mathematical terms, symbols, and notations. It employs forming concepts, comparing and contrasting concepts, and using a graphic organizer.
- ◆ **Puzzling Problems** offers a nonthreatening environment in which students can approach and engage in contextual problem solving while working cooperatively or independently.

Problem-Solving Process

———■———

Overview

"Problem solving means engaging in a task for which the solution method is not known in advance" (NCTM, 2005, p. 52).

The first Standard for Mathematical Practice is "Make sense of problems and persevere in solving them" (Common Core State Standards Initiative, 2012b). Problem solving has traditionally been a challenge for many students, whether in the primary grades or in high school. Knowing "how to teach" problem solving can be an equal challenge for the teacher. One of the difficulties when facilitating problem solving lies in the variety of problems that students encounter as well as the multiple strategies that can be applied to solving them. Another obstacle facing teachers and students is the reading that is required for "making sense of problems." For some students, this is the first roadblock in finding that "entry point" to engage in the problem.

In *Principles and Standards for School Mathematics*, NCTM goes on to state that students should be able to do the following:

- ◆ build new mathematical knowledge through problem solving
- ◆ solve problems that arise in mathematics and in other contexts
- ◆ apply and adapt a variety of appropriate strategies to solve problems
- ◆ monitor and reflect on the process of mathematical problem solving. (NCTM, 2005, p. 116)

Probably the most universally recognized "problem-solving process" can be attributed to George Pôlya, the Hungarian mathematician who came to America in 1940 and published *How to Solve It* in 1943. *How to Solve It* is a small book in which Pôlya describes several methods for solving problems, not just problems in mathematics. As a result of Pôlya's work the following "four-step" plan has become universally used in problem solving:

- ◆ understand the problem
- ◆ devise a plan

♦ carry out the plan
♦ review or extend the work

These four steps are fluid, as illustrated by the graphical adaptation of Pôlya's plan:

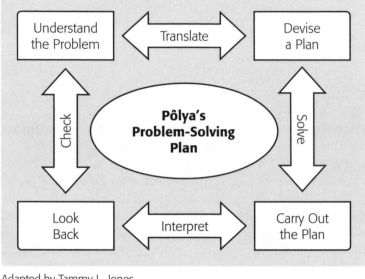

Adapted by Tammy L. Jones
TLJ Consulting Group

If you cannot devise an effective plan, back up and check for understanding of the problem. Once you have reached a solution, look back and reflect to check for the reasonableness of the answer. These four steps have been adapted as illustrated and defined below in a five-step process.

Directions

The following is a problem-solving process that can be used to assist students in making sense of problems **(Practice #1)** as well as decontextualizing and contextualizing word problems **(Practice #2)**. The process also requires students to construct viable arguments **(Practice #3)** as they formulate their own ideas about the meaning of the problem and make predictions about the outcome. Once they obtain a solution, students compare it to the prediction to determine the reasonableness of the solution. By following explicit steps to unpack the problem, students are able to begin the process with minimal to no teacher guidance and complete the initial steps. This eliminates the blank piece of paper or the famous "I don't know" answer. Using a consistent process over time will assist students in becoming better problem solvers. While this process may not always fit every problem, it does help students develop a systematic approach to finding the entry point into various tasks.

Five-Step Problem-Solving Process

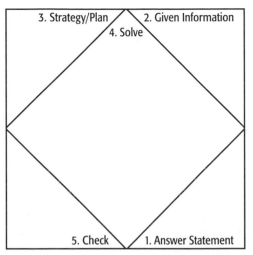

A reproducible version of this tool is available in Appendix A (pp. 103–104).

1. **Answer Statement**
   a. The question usually appears as the last sentence of the problem. Students can cover the other information and focus on the last line to determine what the problem is asking. (If the question is not here, students can check each preceding line until it is found.)
   b. Students write the question as an answer statement and leave a blank for the solution.
2. **Given Information**
   a. Students use the same process of viewing each sentence separately, covering everything else.
   b. Students determine and record relevant information from the problem.
3. **Strategy/Plan**
   a. Students use this space to state additional ideas they have about the problem, such as other information they know about the problem, possible strategies for getting started, estimations for the solution, constraints, or predictions.
   b. This is the section that allows students to formulate their own ideas about the problem and provides a place for them to create their own meaning about what is being asked.
4. **Solve**
   a. Students select a strategy (translate verbal statements into mathematical statements, draw a picture, make a table, etc.) and solve.
   b. Students can compare their solution to the estimation to determine the reasonableness of their answer.

5. Check

    a. Students check their answers by substitution or by using another method to justify.

    b. Once the answer has been checked, students write the answer in the blank from step #1.

——————■——————

Common Core State Standards for Mathematics Addressed
Primary:

Describe and compare measurable attributes.

CCSS.Math.Content.K.MD.A.1 Describe measurable attributes of objects, such as length or weight. Describe several measurable attributes of a single object.

CCSS.Math.Content.K.MD.A.2 Directly compare two objects with a measurable attribute in common, to see which object has "more of"/"less of" the attribute, and describe the difference. *For example, directly compare the heights of two children and describe one child as taller/shorter.*

Measure lengths indirectly and by iterating length units.

CCSS.Math.Content.1.MD.A.1 Order three objects by length; compare the lengths of two objects indirectly by using a third object.

CCSS.Math.Content.1.MD.A.2 Express the length of an object as a whole number of length units, by laying multiple copies of a shorter object (the length unit) end to end; understand that the length measurement of an object is the number of same-size length units that span it with no gaps or overlaps. *Limit to contexts where the object being measured is spanned by a whole number of length units with no gaps or overlaps.*

Relate addition and subtraction to length.

CCSS.Math.Content.2.MD.B.5 Use addition and subtraction within 100 to solve word problems involving lengths that are given in the same units, e.g., by using drawings (such as drawings of rulers) and equations with a symbol for the unknown number to represent the problem.

CCSS.Math.Content.2.MD.B.6. Represent whole numbers as lengths from 0 on a number line diagram with equally spaced points corresponding to the numbers 0, 1, 2, . . . , and represent whole-number sums and differences within 100 on a number line diagram.

Elementary:

Geometric measurement: understand concepts of area and relate area to multiplication and to addition.

CCSS.Math.Content.3.MD.C.7.b Multiply side lengths to find areas of rectangles with whole-number side lengths in the context of solving real-world and mathematical problems, and represent whole-number products as rectangular areas in mathematical reasoning.

Geometric measurement: recognize perimeter.
CCSS.Math.Content.3.MD.D.8. Solve real-world and mathematical problems involving perimeters of polygons, including finding the perimeter given the side lengths, finding an unknown side length, and exhibiting rectangles with the same perimeter and different areas or with the same area and different perimeters.

Solve problems involving measurement and conversion of measurements.
CCSS.Math.Content.4.MD.A.3. Apply the area and perimeter formulas for rectangles in real-world and mathematical problems. *For example, find the width of a rectangular room given the area of the flooring and the length, by viewing the area formula as a multiplication equation with an unknown factor.*

(Common Core State Standards Initiative, 2012a)

Primary Example

Children need experiences in measurements in order to build "measurement landmarks" for them to use later. The first step in understanding measurement is found in the kindergarten cluster, "Describe and compare measurable attributes." Children first need to understand that objects have measureable attributes. Give children a sheet of writing paper and ask them to tell you about it or describe what they see. They will probably tell you its color, maybe its shape, and describe what they see on it. They might even pick it up and tell you it is "floppy" and light. If you give them a second piece of paper, maybe an index card or a piece of construction paper, they can now relate the second piece of paper to the first. Again ask them to tell you what they see. They will again describe its color, shape, what is on the piece of paper, and so on. But now they will begin to describe some relative ideas: The construction paper is bigger than the writing paper. The index card is smaller than the construction paper. The construction paper is blue and the index card is white. Now you can begin the discussion of what is a measurable attribute and what is not.

In the CCSSM, the idea of measurement begins with understanding what is a measurable attribute and comparing those attributes in kindergarten. Understanding how to measure length and using nonstandard units of measurement occurs in the first grade. In addition, students order objects by their lengths. In second grade, students measure objects using inches, feet, centimeters, and meters. They then use those measurements to solve problems. The following problems reflect this progression of learning. The problems are foundational and as such do not incorporate the graphic organizer initially.

Guided Facilitation

Students will be given two or three of the following with which they will identify measurable attributes, compare and order, measure, and make calculations based upon their measurements: a piece of primary or notebook paper, an index card, a piece of construction paper, a piece of poster board, etc.

 NOTE: Before having the students answer the questions below, have a conversation with the class to come to an agreement on which side of the objects you are comparing or measuring.

1. Ask the students to determine which object is the longest. Have them explain their thinking and their reasoning.
2. Ask the students to determine which object is the shortest. Have them explain their thinking and their reasoning.
3. Ask students to put the objects in order from longest to shortest. Have a walk-about review in which the students walk around the room and check each other's work. Have them tell why they think each arrangement is correct or incorrect.
4. Ask the students to put the objects in order from shortest to longest. Again, do a walk-about review.
5. Ask students to compare the objects using another measurable attribute and to tell what attribute they used.
6. Have students find three objects in the classroom that they can compare using measurable attributes.

Problem Statement

Patrick and Jamal measured a piece of paper to completely cover Mrs. Jones's bulletin board. It was 52 inches long. It was the same width as her board. They measured her bulletin board and found out it was only 38 inches long. How much do Jamal and Patrick need to cut off the length of the paper so it will fit Mrs. Jones's bulletin board?

1. **Answer Statement**
    Have the students look for the question mark to find the question. Discuss the question so they understand how to rephrase it as a statement, such as "Jamal and Patrick need to cut off _____ inches."

2. **Given Information**
    Guide students to incorporate a drawing to aid in their identifying the measurable attribute of the object. Check for appropriate labeling of units.

3. **Strategy/Plan**
    This is the place in the problem-solving process that most students encounter difficulty. In the primary grades, students either "put together," "compose," "add," or create a sum so they have more. Or they "take apart," "decompose," "subtract," or find the difference and have less. So the question to ask the students is "Will you have more paper or less paper once you cut some off?" Since there will be less paper, subtraction is required. This can also be framed as adding on for some students. That strategy would also certainly be acceptable.

4. **Solve**
    In the following example, the student chose to model the subtraction with base-ten materials.

5. **Check**
    This is an extremely important step in the problem-solving process. This is where students can check to see if their answer is reasonable and if it does answer the question being asked. When checking their work, students can see how addition and subtraction are inverse operations.

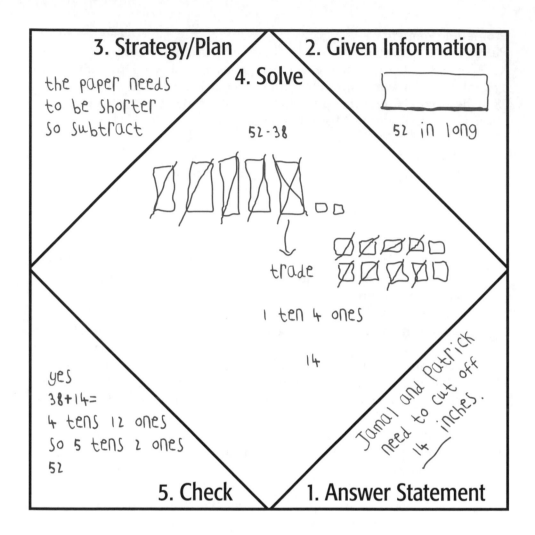

Ideas for Implementing the Five-Step Process Template

- ◆ Individual: Each student is assigned a problem and completes the chart individually as classwork or homework.
- ◆ Individual/Pairs: Students are given a completed chart and must create the problem scenario.
- ◆ Individual/Pairs: Work three or four problems using the five-step process. Cut the steps of each problem into individual strips and place in an envelope. Give students the envelope and ask them to reassemble the strips to form the problems and solution pathways.
- ◆ Individual/Pairs: Give students a completed chart that contains errors and have them identify the errors and make corrections.
- ◆ Partner Pairs: Think-Pair-Share. Allow an initial period of time for each student to read and understand the problem. Then allow partners to discuss and solve the problem together. Students should be prepared to explain their solution to the class.

- ◆ Partner Pairs: Same as previous idea, except that students must solve the problem from two solution pathways.
- ◆ Partner Pairs: Each partner completes steps 1-4 of their individually assigned problem. Partners will then exchange papers and complete step 5 by checking the answer.
- ◆ Small Group: Each student begins with a problem and does step 1. Upon completion of that step, students hand their paper to the next person in a clockwise (or counterclockwise) rotation. Each student then completes the next step in the problem. The process continues for three more steps until all of the steps of the process have been completed.

Elementary Example

Children need experiences in measurements in order to build "measurement landmarks" for them to use later. These landmarks were first encountered in the primary grades. Students in the elementary grades still need to experience measurements of various types. The concepts of perimeter and area are introduced formally in third grade. These concepts are further developed in grade 4 and then expanded to volume in grade 5. Students can often make sense of solving problems involving geometric figures and measurements because they can touch, see, measure, model, and manipulate the figures.

Guided Facilitation

Problem Statement

Patrick and Jamal measured a piece of paper to completely cover Mrs. Jones's bulletin board. The paper was 52 inches long and had the same width as the bulletin board. They measured the board and found out it was 48 inches long and 48 inches wide. What shape is Mrs. Jones's bulletin board? How do you know?

   If the boys are going to put a border around the bulletin board, how much border will they need? If the border is 2 inches wide, how much area will be left on the bulletin board for Mrs. Jones to hang student work? How did you think about that?

1. **Answer Statement**
   Have the students look for the question mark to find the question. Discuss the questions so they understand there are multiple questions to answer. Guide them to rephrase the questions as statements, such as "The shape of Mrs. Jones's bulletin board is a _____ ," "The boys need _____ inches of border to go around the bulletin board," and "There will be _____ square inches of board space left."

NOTE: Step 1 is a good example to discuss different types of questions that can be asked in a problem and what is required to arrive at a solution.

2. **Given Information**

   Guide students to incorporate a drawing to aid in identifying the shape of the bulletin board. Check for appropriate labeling of units and their drawing to get an idea of their spatial sense. The only information the students really need to know for perimeter is that the board is a 48-inch square. An interesting discussion could develop about how to put the border on the board. Does it overlap or not? This opens up the possibility for more than one answer.

3. **Strategy/Plan**

   For the first piece of the problem, students will simply state verbally what they drew. They may go on to state their reason here. This is a good place to check students' understanding of what is "needed" information for this piece of the problem versus what is not needed for this one question. Students should realize that for perimeter they are simply adding the four sides, or using multiplication for efficiency. In the following example, the student commented only about the border, not the strategy she would employ to solve the problem. The students' ability to articulate the strategy they used needs to be monitored very carefully.

4. **Solve**

   Students experience a solution that does not require the traditional arithmetic computation. For this solution, the student was required to make an observation based upon known facts and prior knowledge about geometric figures. Not all math problems have numerical answers. Students can use multiple strategies for solving the second part of this problem. The example shows how the student multiplied by applying base-ten principles and not the standard algorithm. The student went on to convert to feet, which was not required, but the number of inches seemed unwieldy, so she chose to convert the measurement so it would make sense to her.

5. **Check**

   This is an interesting problem in which to observe students' strategies for checking their solutions. This student, who had converted from inches to feet without needing to, used that conversion as a check for the reasonableness of her answer. There was no mention made in the student's work of the square inches (area) left on the bulletin board for Mrs. Jones to hang student work. Being able to convert within systems, especially between square inches and square feet, is a challenging concept for students to understand. This might have been beyond this student's experiences.

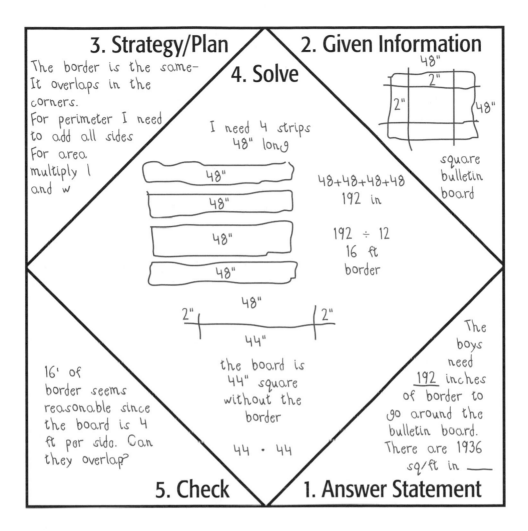

For some students, using three of the templates might better facilitate their beginning to work with a multi-step problem.

Ideas for Implementing the Five-Step Process Template

- ◆ Individual: Each student is assigned a problem and completes the chart individually as classwork or homework.
- ◆ Individual/Pairs: Students are given a completed chart and must create the problem scenario.
- ◆ Individual/Pairs: Work three or four problems using the five-step process. Cut the steps of each problem into individual strips and place in an envelope. Give students the envelope and ask them to reassemble the strips to form the problems and solution pathways.
- ◆ Individual/Pairs: Give students a completed chart that contains errors and have them identify the errors and make corrections.
- ◆ Partner Pairs: Think-Pair-Share. Allow an initial period of time for each student to read and understand the problem. Then allow

partners to discuss and solve the problem together. Students should be prepared to explain their solution to the class.

♦ Partner Pairs: Same as above, except that students must solve the problem from two solution pathways.

♦ Partner Pairs: Each partner completes steps 1-4 of their individually assigned problem. Partners will then exchange papers and complete step 5 by checking the answer.

♦ Small Group: Each student begins with a problem and does step 1. Upon completion of that step, students hand their paper to the next person in a clockwise (or counterclockwise) rotation. Each student then completes the next step in the problem. The process continues for three more steps until all of the steps of the process have been completed.

Visual Vocabulary

Overview

Building mathematical vocabulary is essential, not just for English Language Learners but for all students. Vocabulary is the foundation upon which mathematical understandings develop. Precise use of mathematical vocabulary, symbols, and notations is foundational to successfully implementing all of the Standards for Mathematical Practice. This activity involves students representing their understanding of vocabulary words, phrases, and symbols. The idea was adapted from a lesson shared by Julia Hayes, Newport News, Virginia.

Directions

- Teams will be given a card identifying a math-related word or phrase. If the classroom has a topical word wall, these words or phrases will come from there.
- Teams will illustrate the concept or meaning of the word or phrase without using numbers, variables, or other words. This is *not* Pictionary®: the illustrations should convey meaning, not clues for "guessing the word."
- A gallery walk will be conducted to identify the words. The drawings can be numbered and the students can record the number and the word or phrase they believe is being represented.
- Drawings will be posted. Placing these with the words from the word wall will allow students to continue working with these throughout the next unit as well. Students could also replicate these in their student mathematics glossary they are developing.

Common Core State Standards for Mathematics Addressed
Identify and describe shapes.
CCSS.Math.Content.K.G.A.2 Correctly name shapes regardless of their orientations or overall size.

Reason with shapes and their attributes.

CCSS.Math.Content.1.G.A.3 Partition circles and rectangles into two and four equal shares, describe the shares using the words *halves, fourths,* and *quarters,* and use the phrases *half of, fourth of,* and *quarter of.* Describe the whole as two of, or four of the shares. Understand for these examples that decomposing into more equal shares creates smaller shares.

Reason with shapes and their attributes.

CCSS.Math.Content.2.G.A.3 Partition circles and rectangles into two, three, or four equal shares, describe the shares using the words halves, thirds, half of, a third of, etc., and describe the whole as two halves, three thirds, four fourths. Recognize that equal shares of identical wholes need not have the same shape.

Reason with shapes and their attributes.

CCSS.Math.Content.3.G.A.2 Partition shapes into parts with equal areas. Express the area of each part as a unit fraction of the whole. *For example, partition a shape into 4 parts with equal area, and describe the area of each part as ¼ of the area of the shape.*

Develop understanding of fractions as numbers.

CCSS.Math.Content.3.NF.A.1 Understand a fraction $1/b$ as the quantity formed by 1 part when *a* whole is partitioned into *b* equal parts; understand a fraction a/b as the quantity formed by a parts of size $1/b$.

(Common Core State Standards Initiative, 2012a)

Examples

The examples below illustrate two different math words or phrases.

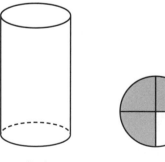

Cylinder   Fraction

Guided Facilitation

Assessment Activity

1. Upon completing the vocabulary illustration activity, create a set of cards displaying the vocabulary word or phrase, a visual representation of the word or phrase, and its definition. See the examples below.
2. Give each student (or group of students) a set of cards.
3. Students must match their cards appropriately.

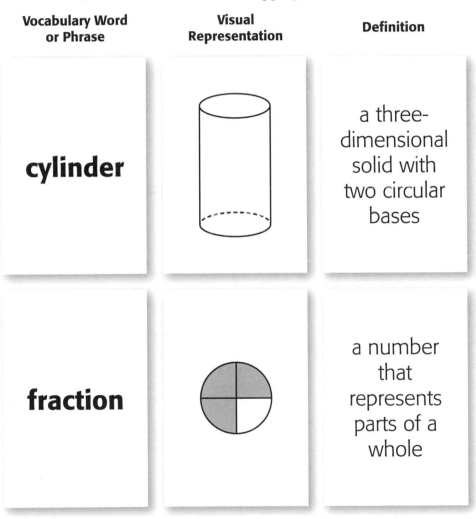

Vocabulary Word or Phrase	Visual Representation	Definition
cylinder		a three-dimensional solid with two circular bases
fraction		a number that represents parts of a whole

Extension Activity

1. Once the students have matched their cards correctly, they will record the vocabulary word or phrase, the visual representation of the word or phrase, and its definition using a vocabulary concept map, such as a Frayer model.

2. Students will then define characteristics of the word or phrase and create a visual counterexample. (At this point, students are allowed to use numerical, algebraic, or symbolic representations.) See the following examples.

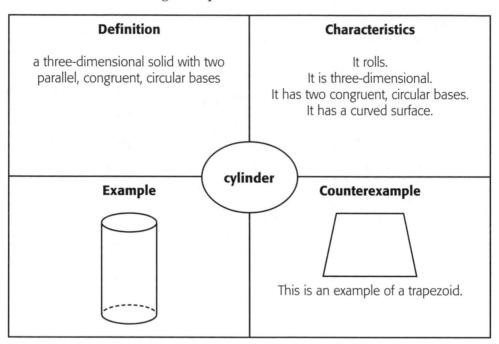

A blank reproducible version of this tool is available in Appendix A (p. 105).

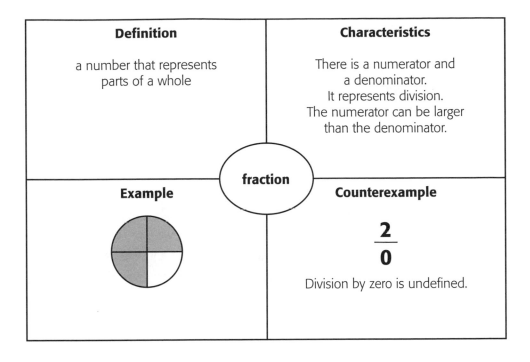

Definition

a number that represents parts of a whole

Characteristics

There is a numerator and a denominator.
It represents division.
The numerator can be larger than the denominator.

fraction

Example

Counterexample

$$\frac{2}{0}$$

Division by zero is undefined.

Puzzling Problems

Overview

Puzzling Problems involves students in cooperative groups working on basic problem solving or a rich task that involves multiple components. The sample tasks that have been developed illustrate the latter. The problems are scaffolded so each subsequent question in some part depends upon the students completing the prior piece. These problems were developed to model what a performance-based assessment at a high cognitive level might look like. Writing is a key component in each of these problems. This is a perfect opportunity for students to employ math journaling or a Mathematician's Notebook to individually record their observations, reasoning, and thoughts as they work through each component of the problems. It also gives them a reference for the next component of the task. Teachers need to remember that just because students can discuss something verbally does not necessarily mean they can capture those thoughts in written words. Writing in mathematics needs to be a natural, daily part of a student's experiences.

This strategy provides students the opportunity to work through mathematical problems collaboratively. The idea was adapted from a lesson shared by Bob Trammel, a math consultant in Indiana.

Directions

1. Enlarge a word problem or task to fit on one sheet of cardstock. Cut the problem into puzzle pieces. The number of pieces can correspond to the number of students per group, or you can give each student multiple pieces of the same puzzle.
2. Give each student a puzzle piece or pieces.
3. Students must match their puzzle pieces to form a problem to solve.
4. As a learning group, students select a strategy to solve the problem.

5. Students solve the problem as a team and submit a solution. The team must be able to construct a viable argument for their solution and document it individually as a journal activity.

If you would like to have the teams solve more than one problem, place additional puzzles around the room and have teams rotate until they have solved the number of problems you determine. Rich tasks can also be broken down so the first problem is the beginning of the task and subsequent problems are the rest of the task.

Common Core State Standards for Mathematics Addressed
Understand addition, and understand subtraction.
CCSS.Math.Content.K.OA.A.1 Represent addition and subtraction with objects, fingers, mental images, drawings, sounds (e.g., claps), acting out situations, verbal explanations, expressions, or equations.
CCSS.Math.Content.K.OA.A.2 Solve addition and subtraction word problems, and add and subtract within 10, e.g., by using objects or drawings to represent the problem.

Represent and solve problems involving addition and subtraction.
CCSS.Math.Content.1.OA.A.1 Use addition and subtraction within 20 to solve word problems involving situations of adding to, taking from, putting together, taking apart, and comparing, with unknowns in all positions, e.g., by using objects, drawings, and equations with a symbol for the unknown number to represent the problem.
CCSS.Math.Content.1.OA.A.2 Solve word problems that call for addition of three whole numbers whose sum is less than or equal to 20, e.g., by using objects, drawings, and equations with a symbol for the unknown number to represent the problem.

Add and subtract within 20.
CCSS.Math.Content.2.OA.B.2 Fluently add and subtract within 20 using mental strategies. By end of Grade 2, know from memory all sums of two one-digit numbers.

Work with equal groups of objects to gain foundations for multiplication.
CCSS.Math.Content.2.OA.C.4 Use addition to find the total number of objects arranged in rectangular arrays with up to 5 rows and up to 5 columns; write an equation to express the total as a sum of equal addends.

Represent and solve problems involving multiplication and division.

CCSS.Math.Content.3.OA.A.1 Interpret products of whole numbers, e.g., interpret 5 × 7 as the total number of objects in 5 groups of 7 objects each. *For example, describe a context in which a total number of objects can be expressed as 5 × 7.*

CCSS.Math.Content.3.OA.A.3 Use multiplication and division within 100 to solve word problems in situations involving equal groups, arrays, and measurement quantities, e.g., by using drawings and equations with a symbol for the unknown number to represent the problem.

Build fractions from unit fractions.

CCSS.Math.Content.4.NF.B.3 Understand a fraction a/b with $a > 1$ as a sum of fractions $1/b$.

CCSS.Math.Content.4.NF.B.3a Understand addition and subtraction of fractions as joining and separating parts referring to the same whole.

Use equivalent fractions as a strategy to add and subtract fractions.

CCSS.Math.Content.5.NF.A.1 Add and subtract fractions with unlike denominators (including mixed numbers) by replacing given fractions with equivalent fractions in such a way as to produce an equivalent sum or difference of fractions with like denominators. *For example,* $2/3 + 5/4 = 8/12 + 15/12 = 23/12$. *(In general,* $a/b + c/d = (ad + bc)/bd$.*)*

(Common Core State Standards Initiative, 2012a)

Primary Example

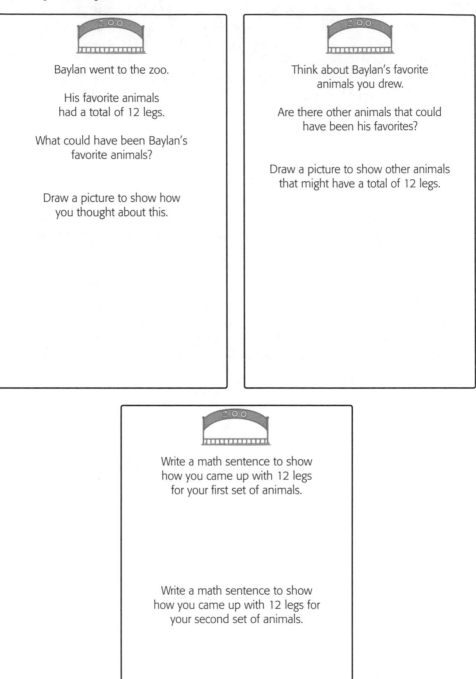

A reproducible version of this tool is available in Appendix A (pp. 106–108).

Grades 2–3 Example

Linda saw two types of butterflies in her grandmother's garden. One type had four spots on its wings. The second type had 5 spots on its wings.

If there were more than one of each type of butterfly in the garden, how many spots could Linda have seen in all?

List at least 10 numbers to show the total number of spots Linda might have seen.

Explain the strategy you used to arrive at the total number of spots possible.

Are there any numbers that could not represent the total number of spots she saw? Why or why not?

A reproducible version of this tool is available in Appendix A (pp. 109–111).

Grades 4–5 Example

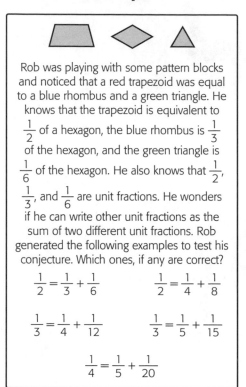

Rob was playing with some pattern blocks and noticed that a red trapezoid was equal to a blue rhombus and a green triangle. He knows that the trapezoid is equivalent to $\frac{1}{2}$ of a hexagon, the blue rhombus is $\frac{1}{3}$ of the hexagon, and the green triangle is $\frac{1}{6}$ of the hexagon. He also knows that $\frac{1}{2}$, $\frac{1}{3}$, and $\frac{1}{6}$ are unit fractions. He wonders if he can write other unit fractions as the sum of two different unit fractions. Rob generated the following examples to test his conjecture. Which ones, if any are correct?

$$\frac{1}{2} = \frac{1}{3} + \frac{1}{6} \qquad \frac{1}{2} = \frac{1}{4} + \frac{1}{8}$$

$$\frac{1}{3} = \frac{1}{4} + \frac{1}{12} \qquad \frac{1}{3} = \frac{1}{5} + \frac{1}{15}$$

$$\frac{1}{4} = \frac{1}{5} + \frac{1}{20}$$

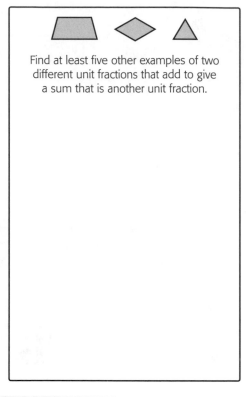

Find at least five other examples of two different unit fractions that add to give a sum that is another unit fraction.

Study all your examples carefully. What pattern do you notice? Write a conjecture for writing any unit fraction as the sum of two different unit fractions.

A reproducible version of this tool is available in Appendix A (pp. 112–114).

Guided Facilitation

Ideas for Implementing the Puzzle Problems
Multiple Representations:
1. For each unit of study, create a set of puzzles. Each puzzle will contain multiple pieces with each piece displaying a different representation of the same problem.
2. Place students in groups of two or three. Each group will receive a set of puzzle pieces.
3. Students must match their pieces appropriately to solve the set of puzzles.

Puzzle Piece Sort (Classification):
1. For each unit of study, create a set of puzzles pieces. Each puzzle piece will display a different mathematical example.
2. Place students in groups of two or three. Each group will receive a set of puzzle pieces.
3. Students must sort and classify all their puzzle pieces.

Equivalency Match:
1. For each unit of study, create a set of puzzles. Each puzzle will comprise two pieces.
2. Each piece of the puzzle will display a different representation of an equivalent quantity.
3. Each pair of students will receive a set of puzzles.
4. Students complete all the puzzles appropriately to show matching equivalencies.

Process Statements:
1. Choose several problems organized around one common concept. Work through each problem.
2. Create a puzzle for each problem. Each piece of the puzzle will display a different step in solving the problem from problem statement to solution.
3. Place students in groups of two or three. Each group will receive a set of puzzles.
4. Students complete all the puzzles appropriately to display the problem, process statements, and solution.

———■———

Strategies for Implementing Combinations of SMPs

The following five Standards for Mathematical Practice, SMP #2, SMP #3, SMP #4, SMP #7, and SMP #8, serve as the door. Your students' mathematics journey continues as they apply these practices, which continue to promote processes, proficiencies, and conceptual understanding in the Common Core mathematics classroom. The implementation of these five practices often occurs in tandem as they are integrated into daily content explorations.

2. Reason abstractly and quantitatively.
Mathematically proficient students make sense of quantities and their relationships in problem situations. They bring two complementary abilities to bear on problems involving quantitative relationships: the ability to *decontextualize*—to abstract a given situation and represent it symbolically and manipulate the representing symbols as if they have a life of their own, without necessarily attending to their referents—and the ability to *contextualize*, to pause as needed during the manipulation process in order to probe into the referents for the symbols involved. Quantitative reasoning entails habits of creating a coherent representation of the problem at hand; considering the units involved; attending to the meaning of quantities, not just how to compute them; and knowing and flexibly using different properties of operations and objects. (Common Core State Standards Initiative, 2012b)

Young children begin with concrete representations of quantities and problems. They use manipulatives, pictures, and other models. As they mature in their number sense development, they begin to think about problems in their head. They begin to reason abstractly and use symbols to represent their reasoning. Students make sense of the numbers and symbols, what they represent, and what labels are attached to them. Students need to be able to move seamlessly between the verbal, the quantitative, and the symbolic representations of numbers and contextual problems.

3. Construct viable arguments and critique the reasoning of others.
Mathematically proficient students understand and use stated assumptions, definitions, and previously established results in constructing arguments. They make conjectures and build a logical progression of statements to explore the truth of their conjectures. They are able to analyze situations by breaking them into cases, and can recognize and use counterexamples. They justify their conclusions, communicate them to others, and respond to the arguments of others. They reason inductively about data, making plausible arguments that take into account the context from which the data arose. Mathematically proficient students are also able to compare

the effectiveness of two plausible arguments, distinguish correct logic or reasoning from that which is flawed, and—if there is a flaw in an argument—explain what it is. Elementary students can construct arguments using concrete referents such as objects, drawings, diagrams, and actions. Such arguments can make sense and be correct, even though they are not generalized or made formal until later grades. Later, students learn to determine domains to which an argument applies. Students at all grades can listen or read the arguments of others, decide whether they make sense, and ask useful questions to clarify or improve the arguments. (Common Core State Standards Initiative, 2012b)

Why? How did you think about that? Why did you choose to use that operation? These and other such probing questions begin to help young children develop an argument for why they reasoned the way they did. Teachers must engage students in mathematical discourse, including conversations, drawings, and writings. Even in the primary grades, students need to be talking about, drawing pictures of, and writing about their mathematics. Students need to hear other students explain their reasoning and be able to critique it and defend their stance. Careful monitoring of the use of precise language, symbols, and figures will ensure that elementary students mature into students who will be able to construct more formal arguments later in their mathematical journey.

4. Model with mathematics.

Mathematically proficient students can apply the mathematics they know to solve problems arising in everyday life, society, and the workplace. In early grades, this might be as simple as writing an addition equation to describe a situation. In middle grades, a student might apply proportional reasoning to plan a school event or analyze a problem in the community. By high school, a student might use geometry to solve a design problem or use a function to describe how one quantity of interest depends on another. Mathematically proficient students who can apply what they know are comfortable making assumptions and approximations to simplify a complicated situation, realizing that these may need revision later. They are able to identify important quantities in a practical situation and map their relationships using such tools as diagrams, two-way tables, graphs, flowcharts and formulas. They can analyze those relationships mathematically to draw conclusions. They routinely interpret their mathematical results in the context of the situation and reflect on whether the results make sense, possibly improving the model if it has not served its purpose. (Common Core State Standards Initiative, 2012b)

Students need experiences with real-world problems so they can see how mathematics can be used to answer questions about their world. Primary students can see how many children in their room like a certain flavor of ice cream, how tall they have grown during the school year, how much more time must pass until lunch, or how much money they have saved in their piggy bank. Mathematics can be used to model each of these situations. Students who can take a contextual situation and translate it into a mathematical representation using math symbols and numbers are well on their way to developing a deeper understanding of the mathematics that they are studying.

7. Look for and make use of structure.

Mathematically proficient students look closely to discern a pattern or structure. Young students, for example, might notice that three and seven more is the same amount as seven and three more, or they may sort a collection of shapes according to how many sides the shapes have. Later, students will see 7×8 equals the well remembered $7 \times 5 + 7 \times 3$, in preparation for learning about the distributive property. In the expression $x^2 + 9x + 14$, older students can see the 14 as 2×7 and the 9 as $2 + 7$. They recognize the significance of an existing line in a geometric figure and can use the strategy of drawing an auxiliary line for solving problems. They also can step back for an overview and shift perspective. They can see complicated things, such as some algebraic expressions, as single objects or as being composed of several objects. For example, they can see $5 - 3(x - y)^2$ as 5 minus a positive number times a square and use that to realize that its value cannot be more than 5 for any real numbers x and y. (Common Core State Standards Initiative, 2012b)

Mathematics is a beautiful language that contains many basic structures and patterns. Students need to have opportunities to discover some of the patterns and structures on their own. Most children will not naturally see all the patterns that exist. Once they have experience with these patterns and structures, young mathematicians use them and what they have learned about mathematics to solve new types of problems they encounter. This is a very important practice as it helps to build the fluency that will be needed as the students move into later mathematical topics.

8. Look for and express regularity in repeated reasoning.

Mathematically proficient students notice if calculations are repeated, and look both for general methods and for shortcuts. Upper elementary students might notice when dividing 25 by 11 that they are repeating the same calculations over and over again, and conclude they have a repeating decimal. By paying attention to the calculation of slope as they repeatedly check whether points are on the line through (1, 2) with slope 3, middle school students might abstract the equation $(y - 2)/(x - 1) = 3$. Noticing the regularity in the way terms cancel when expanding $(x - 1)(x + 1)$, $(x - 1)(x^2 + x + 1)$, and $(x - 1)(x^3 + x^2 + x + 1)$ might lead them to the general formula for the sum of a geometric series. As they work to solve a problem, mathematically proficient students maintain oversight of the process, while attending to the details. They continually evaluate the reasonableness of their intermediate results. (Common Core State Standards Initiative, 2012b)

Even young mathematicians can recognize and build upon prior strategies to make connections between mathematical ideas. They can then apply these connections they have made to new problems and tasks they encounter. Teachers of elementary children of all ages need to provide rich, diverse tasks that will help their students make these connections.

The Strategies

The following five strategies illustrate how these practices permeate each other.

- ◆ **Grid Games** and **Matching Mania** utilize games as a strategy for helping students gain content knowledge and understanding in a nonthreatening atmosphere. Students learn to work in cooperative group situations while practicing and strengthening their problem-solving skills.
- ◆ **The ABC Sum Race** relies on reflective discussions and journaling while students work in cooperative groups to problem-solve various tasks.
- ◆ **Walk This Way** utilizes simulations and role-playing to help students develop understanding of concepts.
- ◆ **What's My Move?** uses reflective discussions and probing questioning to develop a deeper understanding of the content being studied.

The activities in which these strategies are framed simply highlight how each strategy can be used in developing the Standards for Mathematical Practice. These strategies can be adapted to almost any content.

ABC Sum Race

Overview

This activity involves students working in groups to solve problems through a competition. The ABC Sum Race provides an opportunity for students to "construct viable arguments and critique the reasoning of others." Students work both collaboratively and individually while solving problems. Assigning students their problem letter and providing problems at their level can easily differentiate this activity. The problems can be word problems, procedural problems, or computational problems, as desired.

The idea was adapted from a lesson shared by Susie Stark, a math teacher at Rock Island High School in Illinois.

Directions

1. Students are placed in groups of three and asked to assign each person a letter (A, B, and C) and identify a team leader.
2. The team leader comes to the front of the room and gets a task card. The task card contains three problems—problem A, B, and C.
3. Each team member solves the problem that corresponds to the letter he or she represents and records the answer on the scorecard.
4. Once all answers are recorded, the team adds the answers together to get a sum and records it on the scorecard as well. If the solutions cannot be combined, then the SUM column is left blank.
5. The team leader brings the scorecard to the teacher to be checked. If correct, the group moves on to the next game card. If incorrect, the team must redo and resubmit.

Common Core State Standards for Mathematics Addressed
Understand addition, and understand subtraction.
CCSS.Math.Content.K.OA.A.2   Solve addition and subtraction word problems, and add and subtract within 10, e.g., by using objects or drawings to represent the problem.

Represent and solve problems involving addition and subtraction.

CCSS.Math.Content.1.OA.A.1 Use addition and subtraction within 20 to solve word problems involving situations of adding to, taking from, putting together, taking apart, and comparing, with unknowns in all positions, e.g., by using objects, drawings, and equations with a symbol for the unknown number to represent the problem.

Understand place value.

CCSS.Math.Content.1.NBT.B.2 Understand that the two digits of a two-digit number represent amounts of tens and ones. Understand the following as special cases:

CCSS.Math.Content.1.NBT.B.2a 10 can be thought of as a bundle of ten ones—called a "ten."

CCSS.Math.Content.1.NBT.B.2b The numbers from 11 to 19 are composed of a ten and one, two, three, four, five, six, seven, eight, or nine ones.

CCSS.Math.Content.1.NBT.B.2c The numbers 10, 20, 30, 40, 50, 60, 70, 80, 90 refer to one, two, three, four, five, six, seven, eight, or nine tens (and 0 ones).

CCSS.Math.Content.1.NBT.B.3 Compare two two-digit numbers based on meanings of the tens and ones digits, recording the results of comparisons with the symbols >, =, and <.

Use place value understanding and properties of operations to add and subtract.

CCSS.Math.Content.1.NBT.C.4 Add within 100, including adding a two-digit number and a one-digit number, and adding a two-digit number and a multiple of 10, using concrete models or drawings and strategies based on place value, properties of operations, and/or the relationship between addition and subtraction; relate the strategy to a written method and explain the reasoning used. Understand that in adding two-digit numbers, one adds tens and tens, ones and ones; and sometimes it is necessary to compose a ten.

Use place value understanding and properties of operations to add and subtract.

CCSS.Math.Content.2.NBT.B.5 Fluently add and subtract within 100 using strategies based on place value, properties of operations, and/or the relationship between addition and subtraction.

Represent and solve problems involving multiplication and division.

CCSS.Math.Content.3.OA.A.4 Determine the unknown whole number in a multiplication or division equation relating three whole numbers. *For example, determine the unknown number that makes the equation true in each of the equations $8 \times ? = 48, 5 = \_\_ \div 3, 6 \times 6 = ?$*

Reason with shapes and their attributes.

CCSS.Math.Content.3.G.A.1 Understand that shapes in different categories (e.g., rhombuses, rectangles, and others) may share attributes (e.g., having four sides), and that the shared attributes can define a larger category (e.g., quadrilaterals). Recognize rhombuses, rectangles, and squares as examples of quadrilaterals, and draw examples of quadrilaterals that do not belong to any of these subcategories.

Build fractions from unit fractions.

CCSS.Math.Content.4.NF.B.3 Understand a fraction a/b with $a > 1$ as a sum of fractions $1/b$.

CCSS.Math.Content.4.NF.B.3d Solve word problems involving addition and subtraction of fractions referring to the same whole and having like denominators, e.g., by using visual fraction models and equations to represent the problem.

Draw and identify lines and angles, and classify shapes by properties of their lines and angles.

CCSS.Math.Content.4.G.A.3 Recognize a line of symmetry for a two-dimensional figure as a line across the figure such that the figure can be folded along the line into matching parts. Identify line-symmetric figures and draw lines of symmetry.

Use equivalent fractions as a strategy to add and subtract fractions.

CCSS.Math.Content.5.NF.A.2 Solve word problems involving addition and subtraction of fractions referring to the same whole, including cases of unlike denominators, e.g., by using visual fraction models or equations to represent the problem. Use benchmark fractions and number sense of fractions to estimate mentally and assess the reasonableness of answers. *For example, recognize an incorrect result $2/5 + 1/2 = 3/7$ by observing that $3/7 < 1/2$.*

Classify two-dimensional figures into categories based on their properties.

CCSS.Math.Content.5.G.B.3 Understand that attributes belonging to a category of two-dimensional figures also belong to all subcategories of that category. For example, all rectangles have four right angles and squares are rectangles, so all squares have four right angles.

CCSS.Math.Content.5.G.B.4 Classify two-dimensional figures in a hierarchy based on properties.

(Common Core State Standards Initiative, 2012a)

Examples

1.

A. Six buttons are in the basket. Two are yellow. The rest are pink. How many buttons are pink?

B. Leslie has three more stickers than Tammy. Tammy has seven stickers. How many stickers does Leslie have?

C. There are some orange slices on the plate. Baylan ate four orange slices. There is one slice remaining. How many orange slices were on the plate before?

2.

A. How many more are in the right group than in the left group?

B. Patrick has 3 rods and 4 units. How many more does he need to represent the number 38?

C. What number is represented below?

3.

A. $4 \times ? = 20$

B. $? \times 7 = 56$

C. $10 \times 22 = ?$

4.

A. Alex is $2\frac{1}{2}$ years younger than his sister. His sister is 6 years old. How old is Alex?

B. Jamal ran some distance around the school's track. Patrick joins him for the run. They run another $1\frac{1}{4}$ laps around the track. Now Jamal has run $3\frac{1}{2}$ laps total. How many laps did he run before Patrick joined him?

C. A cookie recipe calls for $\frac{1}{3}$ of a cup of butter. Maya only has $\frac{1}{4}$ of a cup of butter. How much does she need to borrow from her neighbor so she can make cookies?

5.

A. I am a 3-D figure called a cube. I have 6 faces. How many vertices do I have?

B. I am a regular, 6-sided, 2-D figure. How many lines of symmetry do I have?

C. I am a quadrilateral that is sometimes a square. What is the measure of one of my interior angles?

A reproducible version of this tool is available in Appendix A (pp. 117–119).

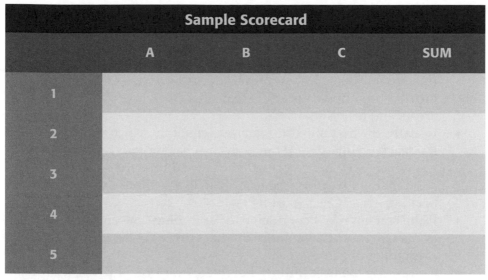

Sample Scorecard			
	A	**B**	**C**	**SUM**
1				
2				
3				
4				
5				

A reproducible version of this tool is available in Appendix A (p. 120).

Answer Key			
	A	**B**	**C**	**SUM**
1	4	10	5	19
2	23	4	43	70
3	5	8	220	233
4	$3\frac{1}{2}$	$2\frac{1}{4}$	$\frac{1}{12}$	$5\frac{5}{6}$
5	8	6	90	104

A reproducible version of this tool is available in Appendix A (p. 121).

Guided Facilitation

♦ The first time through, students must individually solve the problem that corresponds to their letter and record the answer on the answer sheet. If the group leader is sent back to the group with incorrect solutions, the entire team can work together to find the errors and resubmit.

♦ Usually, the first time the team leader submits incorrect answers, the teacher will say that the scorecard has incorrect answers, but not which parts are incorrect. The second time the scorecard is submitted with errors, the teacher will give more specific feedback, such as "Check part B."

♦ If the content is not conducive to "summing" the answers, students will leave that column on the scorecard blank or adapt it to combining like terms, etc.

♦ Color-code the task cards to help keep track of which task card each group is solving. If you have access to a color printer, you can color code the problem numbers on the scorecard.

♦ Have a set time to work or call time when a group reaches the final task card. It is best to call time before the last task card is completed. This will eliminate winners and losers and ensure everyone continues to work until the end of the activity.

Grid Games

Overview

Grid Games is a strategy that creates a nonthreatening environment in which students can practice and build confidence in problem solving and procedural mathematics through a game. Playing the game itself allows students to develop their critical thinking skills while they are building strategies for capturing a cell or blocking their opponent.

Students work problems in order to cover a certain number of the cells on the grid sheet. Students can try to cover 3 in a row, 4 in a row, or even all the cells on the card to win the game as determined by the teacher.

Grid Games was developed by Melisa Rice and is being shared with permission. Additional card sets and topics can be found at www.gridgamesgalore.com.

Directions

Each activity is to be run off on cardstock. The other items necessary to play the games are counters or tiles, a number cube, and a letter cube. Use a foam cube or a cube with stick-on labels to make the letter cube. Use the letters A, B, C, D, E, and F.

1. This game is best played in pairs. Each pair of students needs the Grid Game Board for the Grid Game being played, two student recording sheets, a game sheet, a number cube and a letter cube, and counters of two different colors or double-sided counters. Spinners are also an option instead of the cubes. Provide a number spinner and a letter spinner.

2. Each player rolls the number cube. High roll is Player 1, who begins the game.

3. Player 1 rolls the two cubes and finds the corresponding location on the grid. For example, if Player 1 rolls C5, he locates the fifth square down in the C column.

4. Player 1 then proceeds to answer the question in the C5 square and records the answer on the student recording sheet. If he

answers the question correctly, he places a colored counter on the C5 square on the game board. If he does not answer correctly, Player 2 may answer the question and cover the square.

5. Player 2 then rolls the two cubes, finds the square indicated, and answers the question. As above, if Player 2 answers the question correctly, she covers it with a colored counter. If she misses it, Player 1 may answer the question.

6. Play continues until a player has a specified number of counters in a row, horizontally, vertically, or diagonally, or has covered the entire grid if that was the goal.

7. If a player rolls the cubes and the square has already been covered, the player will roll again.

Common Core State Standards for Mathematics Addressed
Primary:
Identify and describe shapes.

CCSS.Math.Content.K.G.A.2 Correctly name shapes regardless of their orientations or overall size.

CCSS.Math.Content.K.G.A.3 Identify shapes as two-dimensional (lying in a plane, "flat") or three-dimensional ("solid").

Reason with shapes and their attributes.

CCSS.Math.Content.1.G.A.1 Distinguish between defining attributes (e.g., triangles are closed and three-sided) versus non-defining attributes (e.g., color, orientation, overall size); build and draw shapes to possess defining attributes.

CCSS.Math.Content.2.G.A.1 Recognize and draw shapes having specified attributes, such as a given number of angles or a given number of equal faces. Identify triangles, quadrilaterals, pentagons, hexagons, and cubes.

Elementary:
Geometric measurement: understand concepts of area and relate area to multiplication and to addition.

CCSS.Math.Content.3.MD.C.6 Measure areas by counting unit squares (square cm, square m, square in, square ft, and improvised units).

CCSS.Math.Content.3.MD.C.7 Relate area to the operations of multiplication and addition.

CCSS.Math.Content.3.MD.C.7a Find the area of a rectangle with whole-number side lengths by tiling it, and show that the area is the same as would be found by multiplying the side lengths.

CCSS.Math.Content.3.MD.C.7b Multiply side lengths to find areas of rectangles with whole-number side lengths in the context of solving real-world and mathematical problems, and represent whole-number products as rectangular areas in mathematical reasoning.

CCSS.Math.Content.3.MD.C.7c Use tiling to show in a concrete case that the area of a rectangle with whole-number side lengths a and $b + c$ is the sum of $a \times b$ and $a \times c$. Use area models to represent the distributive property in mathematical reasoning.

CCSS.Math.Content.3.MD.C.7d Recognize area as additive. Find areas of rectilinear figures by decomposing them into non-overlapping rectangles and adding the areas of the non-overlapping parts, applying this technique to solve real-world problems.

Solve problems involving measurement and conversion of measurements.

CCSS.Math.Content.4.MD.A.3 Apply the area and perimeter formulas for rectangles in real-world and mathematical problems. *For example, find the width of a rectangular room given the area of the flooring and the length, by viewing the area formula as a multiplication equation with an unknown factor.*

Geometric measurement: understand concepts of volume.

CCSS.Math.Content.5.MD.C.5 Relate volume to the operations of multiplication and addition and solve real-world and mathematical problems involving volume.

CCSS.Math.Content.5.MD.C.5a Find the volume of a right rectangular prism with whole-number side lengths by packing it with unit cubes, and show that the volume is the same as would be found by multiplying the edge lengths, equivalently by multiplying the height by the area of the base. Represent threefold whole-number products as volumes, e.g., to represent the associative property of multiplication.

(Common Core State Standards Initiative, 2012a)

Example: What's My Shape?

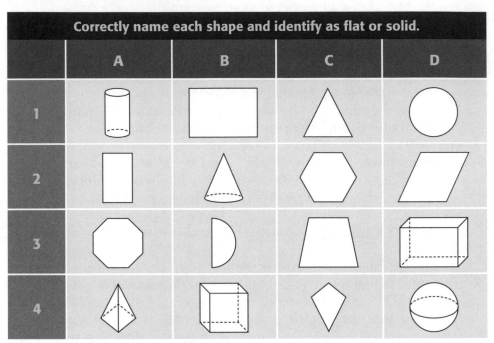

A reproducible version of this tool is available in Appendix A (p. 124).

Example: Perimeter and Area

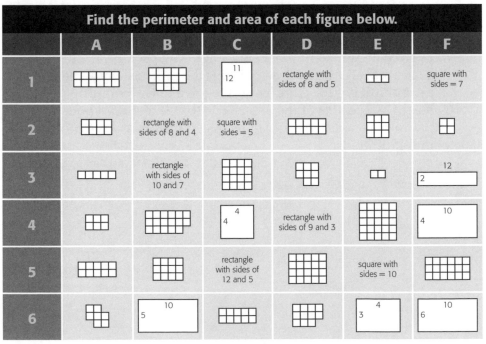

A reproducible version of this tool is available in Appendix A (p. 127).

Guided Facilitation

What's My Shape?

The What's My Shape? Grid Game serves as a nice formative instruction transition for kindergarten. It can be modified, through questioning, to support the standards for second and third grades. What's My Shape? can also serve as a pre-assessment option for intermediate grades as they move into the study of area and volume. Playing the game helps struggling students and students who need some review at any grade level.

Perimeter and Area

The Perimeter and Area Grid Game serves as a nice formative instruction transition for third grade as well as a pre-assessment option for both fourth and fifth grades. Playing the game can also help struggling students and students who need some review.

1. To conserve resources, two grid games could be run off using the front and back of the cardstock. This also allows for differentiation.
2. Putting the grid games in sheet protectors and using two different colors of dry-erase markers eliminates the need for counters.
3. To eliminate the element of chance and to allow students to incorporate strategy, the cubes or spinners are not used. Instead, the students choose where they want to try to claim a cell.
4. If there is a discrepancy in answers, students must "construct a viable argument" or "critique the reasoning of others" to come to consensus.

Matching Mania

Overview

Matching Mania is a strategy that can be applied in multiple ways. As a pre-assessment tool, this strategy allows teachers to gauge where students are in their understanding of a particular topic or skill, their use of the associated vocabulary, and their development in the Standards for Mathematical Practice. Embedded in formative instruction, this strategy becomes a quick and easy transitional activity to check students' understanding of specific content or skills. Matching Mania can also be used as a tool to help students build fluencies. It could even be used as a nonthreatening way to engage students in intervention for skills in which they have gaps.

Students match the problems with the various answers and record on a sheet provided. Each activity is run off on cardstock and cut into pieces. Nothing else is needed. If the objective is to build fluency or check for fluency, give students both sets of cards. Have the students "create a viable argument" for at least five of the matches. Other students' arguments could also be shared and critiqued. To focus on problem solving, give the students only the problem cards. Have them determine the solutions, explain their strategy, and justify their reasoning. They then check their work using the answer cards provided. In cases where there are multiple matches to be made, it is best to initially give the students only one set of cards to match at a time. Later, multiple sets can be used as students' proficiency develops.

Matching Mania was developed by Melisa Rice and is being shared with permission. Additional card sets and topics can be found at www.gridgamesgalore.com.

Directions

1. All student recording sheets are numbered down the left side with the problem number correlating to the problem number found in the upper left corner of the problem cards.

2. Copy each set of cards within the activity on different colored paper or cardstock. This will allow students to easily differentiate the problem cards from the answer cards.
3. Matching Mania requires time in cutting out each activity. You might seek parent volunteers or perhaps student groups that can do this as part of community service hours, or you can have your students cut out the problems and solutions as they work.
4. There are several ways to organize the materials for efficient storage. Use zipper lock quart-size bags to store each set of Matching Mania activity cards. Use gallon bags to store all the individual activity cards, as well as extra recording sheets and the answer key.

Common Core State Standards for Mathematics Addressed
Primary:
Understand addition, and understand subtraction.
CCSS.Math.Content.K.OA.A.5 Fluently add and subtract within 5.

Add and subtract within 20.
CCSS.Math.Content.1.OA.C.6 Add and subtract within 20, demonstrating fluency for addition and subtraction within 10. Use strategies such as counting on; making ten (e.g., $8 + 6 = 8 + 2 + 4 = 10 + 4 = 14$); decomposing a number leading to a ten (e.g., $13 - 4 = 13—3 - 1 = 10 - 1 = 9$); using the relationship between addition and subtraction (e.g., knowing that $8 + 4 = 12$, one knows $12 - 8 = 4$); and creating equivalent but easier or known sums (e.g., adding $6 + 7$ by creating the known equivalent $6 + 6 + 1 = 12 + 1 = 13$).
CCSS.Math.Content.2.OA.B.2 Fluently add and subtract within 20 using mental strategies. By end of grade 2, know from memory all sums of two one-digit numbers.

Elementary:
Understand properties of multiplication and the relationship between multiplication and division.
CCSS.Math.Content.3.OA.B.6 Understand division as an unknown-factor problem. *For example, find 32 ÷ 8 by finding the number that makes 32 when multiplied by 8.*

Gain familiarity with factors and multiples.
CCSS.Math.Content.4.OA.B.4 Find all factor pairs for a whole number in the range 1–100. Recognize that a whole number is a multiple of each of its factors. Determine whether a given whole number in the range 1–100 is a multiple of a given one-digit number. Determine whether a given whole number in the range 1–100 is prime or composite.

Analyze patterns and relationships.

CCSS.Math.Content.5.OA.B.3 Generate two numerical patterns using two given rules. Identify apparent relationships between corresponding terms. Form ordered pairs consisting of corresponding terms from the two patterns, and graph the ordered pairs on a coordinate plane. *For example, given the rule "Add 3" and the starting number 0, and given the rule "Add 6" and the starting number 0, generate terms in the resulting sequences, and observe that the terms in one sequence are twice the corresponding terms in the other sequence. Explain informally why this is so.*

Perform operations with multi-digit whole numbers and with decimals to hundredths.

CCSS.Math.Content.5.NBT.B.6 Find whole-number quotients of whole numbers with up to four-digit dividends and two-digit divisors, using strategies based on place value, the properties of operations, and/or the relationship between multiplication and division. Illustrate and explain the calculation by using equations, rectangular arrays, and/or area models.

Use equivalent fractions as a strategy to add and subtract fractions.

CCSS.Math.Content.5.NF.A.1 Add and subtract fractions with unlike denominators (including mixed numbers) by replacing given fractions with equivalent fractions in such a way as to produce an equivalent sum or difference of fractions with like denominators. *For example,* $2/3 + 5/4 = 8/12 + 15/12 = 23/12.$ *(In general,* $a/b + c/d = {(ad + bc)}/{bd}.)$

Apply and extend previous understandings of multiplication and division.

CCSS.Math.Content.5.NF.B.6 Solve real-world problems involving multiplication of fractions and mixed numbers, e.g., by using visual fraction models or equations to represent the problem.

CCSS.Math.Content.5.NF.B.7 Apply and extend previous understandings of division to divide unit fractions by whole numbers and whole numbers by unit fractions.

(Common Core State Standards Initiative, 2012a)

Example: One-Digit Operations

1	9	5	**2**	6	1
3	8	3	**4**	5	1
5	7	6	**6**	9	9
7	9	7	**8**	2	1
9	5	4	**10**	8	4
11	6	2	**12**	3	1
13	9	8	**14**	9	6
15	6	2	**16**	3	2
17	8	1	**18**	7	5

A reproducible version of this tool is available in Appendix A (pp. 130–132).

A.	R.
sum = 3	sum = 4
B.	Q.
sum = 5	sum = 6
C.	P.
sum = 7	sum = 9
D.	P.
sum = 8	sum = 9
D.	N.
sum = 8	sum = 11
F.	M.
sum = 13	sum = 12
G.	M.
sum = 14	sum = 12
H.	K.
sum = 15	sum = 16
I.	J.
sum = 17	sum = 18

a.
 	
   difference = 0
	g.
	
	   difference = 7

b.
 	
   difference = 1
	f.
	
	   difference = 5

b.
 	
   difference = 1
	f.
	
	   difference = 5

b.
 	
   difference = 1
	e.
	
	   difference = 4

b.
 	
   difference = 1
	e.
	
	   difference = 4

b.
 	
   difference = 1
	e.
	
	   difference = 4

c.
 	
   difference = 2
	e.
	
	   difference = 4

c.
 	
   difference = 2
	e.
	
	   difference = 4

c.
 	
   difference = 2
	d.
	
	   difference = 3

One-Digit Operations		
Numbers	**Sum**	**Difference**
1		
2		
3		
4		
5		
6		
7		
8		
9		
10		
11		
12		
13		
14		
15		
16		
17		
18		

One-Digit Operations		
Numbers	**Sum**	**Difference**
1		
2		
3		
4		
5		
6		
7		
8		
9		
10		
11		
12		
13		
14		
15		
16		
17		
18		

www.gridgamesgalore.com
A reproducible version of this tool is available in Appendix A (p. 133).

Example: Factors and Primes

1 **20**	**2** **56**
3 **36**	**4** **18**
5 **40**	**6** **60**
7 **84**	**8** **35**
9 **28**	**10** **42**
11 **24**	**12** **12**
13 **48**	**14** **32**
15 **45**	**16** **90**
17 **96**	**18** **16**

A. 1, 2, 3, 4, 6, 12	**R.** 1, 5, 7, 35
B. 1, 2, 3, 4, 6, 8, 12, 24, 48	**Q.** 1, 2, 3, 4, 6, 8, 12, 24
C. 1, 2, 4, 7, 14, 28	**P.** 1, 2, 4, 5, 8, 10, 20, 40
D. 1, 2, 4, 8, 16	**O.** 1, 2, 3, 6, 7, 14, 21, 42
E. 1, 2, 3, 4, 6, 7, 12, 14, 21, 28, 42, 84	**N.** 1, 3, 5, 9, 15, 45
F. 1, 2, 4, 8, 16, 32	**M.** 1, 2, 3, 4, 6, 9, 12, 18, 36
G. 1, 2, 3, 4, 6, 8, 12, 16, 24, 32, 48, 96	**L.** 1, 2, 3, 5, 6, 9, 10, 15, 18, 30, 45, 90
H. 1, 2, 4, 5, 10, 20	**K.** 1, 2, 4, 7, 8, 14, 28, 56
I. 1, 2, 3, 6, 9, 18	**J.** 1, 2, 3, 4, 6, 10, 15, 20, 30, 60

a. $2 \times 2 \times 2 \times 7$	r. $2 \times 2 \times 3$
b. $2 \times 2 \times 3 \times 3$	q. $2 \times 2 \times 2 \times 2 \times 3$
c. $2 \times 2 \times 2 \times 3$	p. $2 \times 2 \times 5$
d. $3 \times 3 \times 5$	o. $2 \times 2 \times 2 \times 2 \times 2$
e. $2 \times 2 \times 3 \times 5$	n. $2 \times 2 \times 2 \times 2$
f. $3 \times 3 \times 2$	m. $2 \times 2 \times 3 \times 7$
g. 5×7	l. $3 \times 3 \times 2 \times 5$
h. $2 \times 2 \times 7$	k. $2 \times 2 \times 2 \times 2 \times 2 \times 3$
i. $2 \times 3 \times 7$	j. $2 \times 2 \times 2 \times 5$

Factors and Primes		
Numbers	Factors	Prime Factors
1		
2		
3		
4		
5		
6		
7		
8		
9		
10		
11		
12		
13		
14		
15		
16		
17		
18		

Factors and Primes		
Numbers	Factors	Prime Factors
1		
2		
3		
4		
5		
6		
7		
8		
9		
10		
11		
12		
13		
14		
15		
16		
17		
18		

Example: Operations with Fractions 2

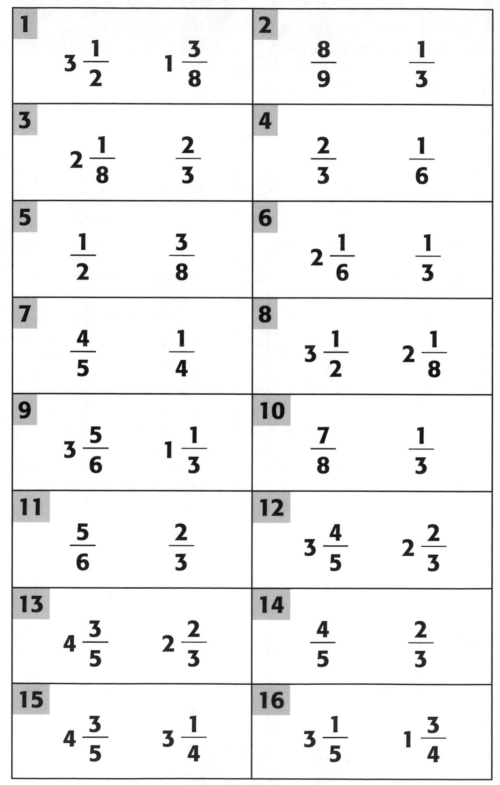

1		2	
$3\frac{1}{2}$ $1\frac{3}{8}$		$\frac{8}{9}$ $\frac{1}{3}$	
3		4	
$2\frac{1}{8}$ $\frac{2}{3}$		$\frac{2}{3}$ $\frac{1}{6}$	
5		6	
$\frac{1}{2}$ $\frac{3}{8}$		$2\frac{1}{6}$ $\frac{1}{3}$	
7		8	
$\frac{4}{5}$ $\frac{1}{4}$		$3\frac{1}{2}$ $2\frac{1}{8}$	
9		10	
$3\frac{5}{6}$ $1\frac{1}{3}$		$\frac{7}{8}$ $\frac{1}{3}$	
11		12	
$\frac{5}{6}$ $\frac{2}{3}$		$3\frac{4}{5}$ $2\frac{2}{3}$	
13		14	
$4\frac{3}{5}$ $2\frac{2}{3}$		$\frac{4}{5}$ $\frac{2}{3}$	
15		16	
$4\frac{3}{5}$ $3\frac{1}{4}$		$3\frac{1}{5}$ $1\frac{3}{4}$	

A. Sum $= 7\dfrac{17}{20}$	**R.** Sum $= 5\dfrac{1}{6}$
B. Sum $= 4\dfrac{19}{20}$	**Q.** Sum $= 1\dfrac{1}{20}$
C. Sum $= \dfrac{7}{8}$	**P.** Sum $= 2\dfrac{5}{6}$
D. Sum $= \dfrac{5}{6}$	**O.** Sum $= 1\dfrac{2}{9}$
E. Sum $= 6\dfrac{7}{15}$	**N.** Sum $= 2\dfrac{19}{24}$
F. Sum $= 5\dfrac{5}{8}$	**M.** Sum $= 7\dfrac{4}{15}$
G. Sum $= 4\dfrac{7}{8}$	**L.** Sum $= 1\dfrac{5}{24}$
H. Sum $= 1\dfrac{1}{2}$	**K.** Sum $= 1\dfrac{7}{15}$

A. Difference $= 2\frac{1}{8}$	**R.** Difference $= 1\frac{14}{15}$
B. Difference $= \frac{1}{2}$	**Q.** Difference $= 2\frac{1}{2}$
C. Difference $= \frac{5}{9}$	**P.** Difference $= 1\frac{1}{2}$
D. Difference $= \frac{1}{8}$	**O.** Difference $= 1\frac{11}{24}$
E. Difference $= \frac{13}{24}$	**N.** Difference $= 1\frac{3}{8}$
F. Difference $= \frac{2}{15}$	**M.** Difference $= \frac{11}{20}$
G. Difference $= \frac{1}{6}$	**L.** Difference $= 1\frac{9}{20}$
H. Difference $= 1\frac{2}{15}$	**K.** Difference $= 1\frac{7}{20}$

a. $$\text{Product} = \frac{1}{9}$$	**p.** $$\text{Product} = 5\frac{1}{9}$$
b. $$\text{Product} = 1\frac{5}{12}$$	**o.** $$\text{Product} = \frac{8}{27}$$
c. $$\text{Product} = 1\frac{4}{9}$$	**n.** $$\text{Product} = 12\frac{4}{15}$$
d. $$\text{Product} = \frac{5}{9}$$	**m.** $$\text{Product} = \frac{3}{16}$$
e. $$\text{Product} = 10\frac{2}{15}$$	**l.** $$\text{Product} = \frac{7}{24}$$
f. $$\text{Product} = \frac{1}{5}$$	**k.** $$\text{Product} = 7\frac{7}{16}$$
g. $$\text{Product} = 14\frac{19}{20}$$	**j.** $$\text{Product} = \frac{8}{15}$$
h. $$\text{Product} = 5\frac{3}{5}$$	**i.** $$\text{Product} = 4\frac{13}{16}$$

a. Quotient $= 1\dfrac{1}{3}$	**p.** Quotient $= 1\dfrac{1}{4}$
b. Quotient $= 2\dfrac{7}{8}$	**o.** Quotient $= 3\dfrac{1}{4}$
c. Quotient $= 1\dfrac{29}{35}$	**n.** Quotient $= 3\dfrac{3}{16}$
d. Quotient $= 2\dfrac{6}{11}$	**m.** Quotient $= 2\dfrac{2}{3}$
e. Quotient $= 4$	**l.** Quotient $= 1\dfrac{1}{5}$
f. Quotient $= 1\dfrac{29}{40}$	**k.** Quotient $= 1\dfrac{11}{17}$
g. Quotient $= 2\dfrac{5}{8}$	**j.** Quotient $= 3\dfrac{1}{5}$
h. Quotient $= 1\dfrac{17}{40}$	**i.** Quotient $= 1\dfrac{27}{65}$

b. **LCD = 6**	**g.** **LCD = 24**
b. **LCD = 6**	**g.** **LCD = 24**
b. **LCD = 6**	**f.** **LCD = 20**
b. **LCD = 6**	**f.** **LCD = 20**
c. **LCD = 8**	**f.** **LCD = 20**
c. **LCD = 8**	**e.** **LCD = 15**
c. **LCD = 8**	**e.** **LCD = 15**
d. **LCD = 9**	**e.** **LCD = 15**

Operations with Fractions 2

Fractions	Sum	Difference	Product	Quotient	LCD
1					
2					
3					
4					
5					
6					
7					
8					
9					
10					
11					
12					
13					
14					
15					
16					

Operations with Fractions 2

Fractions	Sum	Difference	Product	Quotient	LCD
1					
2					
3					
4					
5					
6					
7					
8					
9					
10					
11					
12					
13					
14					
15					
16					

Guided Facilitation

One-Digit Operations

Teachers can use One-Digit Operations Matching Mania as a pre-assessment strategy to gauge where students are in their understanding of addition, subtraction, and the associated vocabulary. Embedded in formative instruction, this strategy becomes a quick and easy transitional activity to check students' understanding of finding sums and differences. Matching Mania can also be used as a tool to help students build mental fluency with sums and differences. Struggling students can engage in Matching Mania as intervention for skills in which they have gaps.

♦ One-Digit Operations Matching Mania consists of eighteen pairs of numbers that can be added or subtracted. Students will find the sum or the difference of the given numbers.
♦ The worksheet, numbers, and the appropriate forms of the answer are listed below:
  • Student recording sheet
  • The number cards
  • The solution cards for the sum
  • The solution cards for the difference
♦ Place students in pairs. Students work as pairs matching the appropriate solutions to each problem and filling out the recording sheet.

Factors and Primes

Teachers can use Factors and Primes Matching Mania as a pre-assessment strategy to gauge where students are in their understanding of multiplication, division, associated vocabulary, and seeing patterns. Embedded in formative instruction, this strategy becomes a quick and easy transitional activity to check students' understanding of finding an unknown factor, determining if a number is prime or composite, and visualizing patterns. Matching Mania can also be used as a tool to help students build mental fluency with multiplication and division as well as support the development of related standards. It can also be a nonthreatening way to engage students in intervention for skills in which they have gaps.

♦ Factors and Primes Matching Mania consists of 18 numbers that can be represented as both the set of factors for a given number as well as the prime factors for that number. Students will find one or both forms of the given number.
♦ The worksheet, numbers, and the appropriate forms of the answer are listed below:
  • Student recording sheet
  • The number cards

- The solution cards as a set of factors
- The solution cards as a set of prime factors
♦ Place students in pairs. Students work as pairs matching the appropriate solutions to each problem and filling out the recording sheet.

Operations with Fractions 2*

Teachers can use Operations with Fractions 2 Matching Mania as a pre-assessment strategy to gauge where students are in their understanding of operating with fractions, determining the least common denominator, and the associated vocabulary. Embedded in formative instruction, this strategy becomes a quick and easy transitional activity to check students' understanding of fraction operations or determining the LCD for two fractions. Matching Mania can also be used as a tool to help students build procedural fluency when operating with fractions as well as support the development of related standards. It can also be a nonthreatening way to engage students in intervention for skills in which they have gaps. (Note: This activity includes dividing fractions by fractions, which is beyond the CCSSM fifth-grade standards.)

♦ Operations with Fractions 2 Matching Mania consists of 16 pairs of fractions and mixed numbers that can be simplified by addition, subtraction, multiplication, and division by using the fractions rules. Students will perform each operation to find the appropriate answer.
♦ The student recording sheet, fraction cards, and the appropriate forms for the answer are listed below:
  - Student recording sheet
  - Fraction pairs (different denominators)
  - Sum of the fraction pairs (common denominators)
  - Difference of the fraction pairs (common denominators)
  - Product of the fraction pairs
  - Quotient of the fraction pairs
  - Least common denominators (LCD)
♦ Place students in pairs. Students work as pairs matching the appropriate solutions to each problem and filling out the recording sheet.

*Grid Games Galore (www.gridgamesgalore.com) features two versions of this activity. This is the second.

Walk This Way

Overview

Walk This Way allows students to use repeated reasoning to investigate mathematical concepts on number lines as well as the Cartesian coordinate plane by physically representing mathematical situations on a life-size graph. Students can walk a number line to represent quantities that are being composed or decomposed as well as quantities in real-world contexts. Number lines need not be limited to whole numbers. Number lines with fractions and decimals can also be explored.

> **NOTE:** The emphasis of this activity is to have students physically explore composing and decomposing numbers as well as ordering and comparing quantities. Graphing ordered pairs is also investigated.

Directions

1. In the primary grades, make a large number line on which students can walk. A student can be assigned a starting number and then can walk "1 more," "1 less," "3 more," "how many steps to get to 10," "add 5 more and then add 3 more," "subtract 3," and even model a story problem. The other children can be following on individual number lines and recording their appropriate mathematical sentences or equations. Number lines can be marked in 10s to aid counting by 10.

2. Students can skip count on the number line by skipping or hopping by 2, by 3, and so on. Two students can skip count at the same time by skipping on opposite sides of the number line. A student can start at 0 and skip by 2s while another student starts at zero and skips by 3s; their classmates can investigate when the students would land on the same number and why. This activity can later be expanded to include multiplication as repeated addition and observing the different factors for a given product. Students can also investigate the commutative property of addition and the

associative property of addition by standing on opposite sides of the number line and walking the addends in different orders.

3. Even and odd numbers can be investigated on the number line. Students can conjecture how to add and have an even sum, or add and have an odd sum. The number line provides a visual model for justifying why the conjectures are true.

4. Numbers can be compared and ordered on the number line. Fractions and decimals can also be represented on number lines to aid in comparing, ordering, and operating with the numbers. A number line could be made to model a ruler to help students understand measuring in ½ units, ¼ units, and so on. Number lines can be created to represent different unit fraction values.

5. A large Cartesian coordinate plane will be needed so the students can physically graph coordinates. This could be a painter's tarp that has been prepped, the tiles on the classroom floor with the x- and y-axes marked, or the football field with the axes drawn. Prepare by drawing a coordinate plane with $D = \{0 \leq x \leq 25\}$ and $R = \{0 \leq y \leq 25\}$. Be sure to label the axes.

Common Core State Standards for Mathematics Addressed

Know number names and the count sequence.

CCSS.Math.Content.K.CC.A.1 Count to 100 by ones and by tens.

CCSS.Math.Content.K.CC.A.2 Count forward beginning from a given number within the known sequence (instead of having to begin at 1).

Understand addition, and understand subtraction.

CCSS.Math.Content.K.OA.A.1 Represent addition and subtraction with objects, fingers, mental images, drawings, sounds (e.g., claps), acting out situations, verbal explanations, expressions, or equations.

CCSS.Math.Content.K.OA.A.2 Solve addition and subtraction word problems, and add and subtract within 10, e.g., by using objects or drawings to represent the problem.

CCSS.Math.Content.K.OA.A.3 Decompose numbers less than or equal to 10 into pairs in more than one way, e.g., by using objects or drawings, and record each decomposition by a drawing or equation (e.g., 5 = 2 + 3 and 5 = 4 + 1).

CCSS.Math.Content.K.OA.A.4 For any number from 1 to 9, find the number that makes 10 when added to the given number, e.g., by using objects or drawings, and record the answer with a drawing or equation.

CCSS.Math.Content.K.OA.A.5 Fluently add and subtract within 5.

Represent and solve problems involving addition and subtraction.

CCSS.Math.Content.1.OA.A.1 Use addition and subtraction within 20 to solve word problems involving situations of adding to, taking from, putting together, taking apart, and comparing, with unknowns in all positions, e.g., by using objects, drawings, and equations with a symbol for the unknown number to represent the problem.

CCSS.Math.Content.1.OA.A.2 Solve word problems that call for addition of three whole numbers whose sum is less than or equal to 20, e.g., by using objects, drawings, and equations with a symbol for the unknown number to represent the problem.

Understand and apply properties of operations and the relationship between addition and subtraction.

CCSS.Math.Content.1.OA.B.3 Apply properties of operations as strategies to add and subtract. *Examples: If 8 + 3 = 11 is known, then 3 + 8 = 11 is also known. (Commutative property of addition.) To add 2 + 6 + 4, the second two numbers can be added to make a ten, so 2 + 6 + 4 = 2 + 10 = 12. (Associative property of addition.)*

CCSS.Math.Content.1.OA.B.4 Understand subtraction as an unknown-addend problem. *For example, subtract 10 − 8 by finding the number that makes 10 when added to 8. Add and subtract within 20.*

Represent and solve problems involving addition and subtraction.

CCSS.Math.Content.2.OA.A.1 Use addition and subtraction within 100 to solve one- and two-step word problems involving situations of adding to, taking from, putting together, taking apart, and comparing, with unknowns in all positions, e.g., by using drawings and equations with a symbol for the unknown number to represent the problem.

Work with equal groups of objects to gain foundations for multiplication.

CCSS.Math.Content.2.OA.C.3 Determine whether a group of objects (up to 20) has an odd or even number of members, e.g., by pairing objects or counting them by 2s; write an equation to express an even number as a sum of two equal addends.

Relate addition and subtraction to length.

CCSS.Math.Content.2.MD.B.6 Represent whole numbers as lengths from 0 on a number line diagram with equally spaced points corresponding to the numbers 0, 1, 2, . . . , and represent whole-number sums and differences within 100 on a number line diagram.

Solve problems involving the four operations, and identify and explain patterns in arithmetic.

CCSS.Math.Content.3.OA.D.9 Identify arithmetic patterns (including patterns in the addition table or multiplication table), and explain them using properties of operations. *For example, observe that 4 times a number is always even, and explain why 4 times a number can be decomposed into two equal addends.*

Represent and interpret data.

CCSS.Math.Content.3.MD.B.4 Generate measurement data by measuring lengths using rulers marked with halves and fourths of an inch. Show the data by making a line plot, where the horizontal scale is marked off in appropriate units—whole numbers, halves, or quarters.

Extend understanding of fraction equivalence and ordering.

CCSS.Math.Content.4.NF.A.1 Explain why a fraction a/b is equivalent to a fraction $(n \times a)/(n \times b)$ by using visual fraction models, with attention to how the number and size of the parts differ even though the two fractions themselves are the same size. Use this principle to recognize and generate equivalent fractions.

CCSS.Math.Content.4.NF.A.2 Compare two fractions with different numerators and different denominators, e.g., by creating common denominators or numerators, or by comparing to a benchmark fraction such as ½. Recognize that comparisons are valid only when the two fractions refer to the same whole. Record the results of comparisons with symbols >, =, or <, and justify the conclusions, e.g., by using a visual fraction model.

Understand decimal notation for fractions, and compare decimal fractions.

CCSS.Math.Content.4.NF.C.6 Use decimal notation for fractions with denominators 10 or 100. *For example, rewrite 0.62 as $62/100$; describe a length as 0.62 meters; locate 0.62 on a number line diagram.*

CCSS.Math.Content.4.NF.C.7 Compare two decimals to hundredths by reasoning about their size. Recognize that comparisons are valid only when the two decimals refer to the same whole. Record the results of comparisons with the symbols >, =, or <, and justify the conclusions, e.g., by using a visual model.

Graph points on the coordinate plane to solve real-world and mathematical problems.

CCSS.Math.Content.5.G.A.1 Use a pair of perpendicular number lines, called axes, to define a coordinate system, with the intersection of the lines (the origin) arranged to coincide with the 0 on each line and a given point in the plane located by using an ordered pair of numbers, called its coordinates. Understand that the first number indicates how far to travel from the origin in the direction of one axis, and the second number indicates how far to travel in the direction of the second axis, with the convention that the names of the two axes and the coordinates correspond (e.g., x-axis and x-coordinate, y-axis and y-coordinate).

CCSS.Math.Content.5.G.A.2 Represent real-world and mathematical
    problems by graphing points in the first quadrant of the coordinate
    plane, and interpret coordinate values of points in the context of the
    situation.

(Common Core State Standards Initiative, 2012a)

What's My Move?

―――――――――■―――――――――

Overview

This activity is adapted from universal problems such as Traffic Jam or Tower of Hanoi. The basic setup below shows two people on each side of the table with an open space on one end and a "dead end" on the other. The objective is to move all the players from one side of the table to the other side and vice versa in the fewest moves possible.

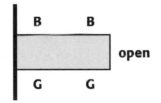

Directions

1. Only *one* player may move at a time.
2. A player may only "slide" (move) into an *open* space.
3. Players must continue moving in the same direction they began.
4. A player may only "jump" (go around) a player from the *other* team. For example, in the diagram above, a B can only jump around a G and vice versa.

> **NOTE:** If there are no viable moves, the players must start over. Many groups will try to "undo" moves rather than restarting the activity. This is not allowed.

―――――――――■―――――――――

Common Core State Standards for Mathematics Addressed
Primary:
Count to tell the number of objects.
CCSS.Math.Content.K.CC.B.4 Understand the relationship between numbers and quantities; connect counting to cardinality.

CCSS.Math.Content.K.CC.B.4a When counting objects, say the number names in the standard order, pairing each object with one and only one number name and each number name with one and only one object.

CCSS.Math.Content.K.CC.B.4b Understand that the last number name said tells the number of objects counted. The number of objects is the same regardless of their arrangement or the order in which they were counted.

CCSS.Math.Content.K.CC.B.4c Understand that each successive number name refers to a quantity that is one larger.

CCSS.Math.Content.K.CC.B.5 Count to answer "how many?" questions about as many as 20 things arranged in a line, a rectangular array, or a circle, or as many as 10 things in a scattered configuration; given a number from 1–20, count out that many objects.

Identify and describe shapes.

CCSS.Math.Content.K.G.A.1 Describe objects in the environment using names of shapes, and describe the relative positions of these objects using terms such as *above*, *below*, *beside*, *in front of*, *behind*, and *next to*.

Represent and solve problems involving addition and subtraction.

CCSS.Math.Content.1.OA.A.1 Use addition and subtraction within 20 to solve word problems involving situations of adding to, taking from, putting together, taking apart, and comparing, with unknowns in all positions, e.g., by using objects, drawings, and equations with a symbol for the unknown number to represent the problem.

CCSS.Math.Content.1.OA.A.2 Solve word problems that call for addition of three whole numbers whose sum is less than or equal to 20, e.g., by using objects, drawings, and equations with a symbol for the unknown number to represent the problem.

Extend the counting sequence.

CCSS.Math.Content.1.NBT.A.1 Count to 120, starting at any number less than 120. In this range, read and write numerals and represent a number of objects with a written numeral.

Represent and interpret data.

CCSS.Math.Content.1.MD.C.4 Organize, represent, and interpret data with up to three categories; ask and answer questions about the total number of data points, how many in each category, and how many more or less are in one category than in another.

Represent and solve problems involving addition and subtraction.

CCSS.Math.Content.2.OA.A.1 Use addition and subtraction within 100 to solve one- and two-step word problems involving situations of adding to, taking from, putting together, taking apart, and comparing, with unknowns in all positions, e.g., by using drawings and equations with a symbol for the unknown number to represent the problem.

Work with equal groups of objects to gain foundations for multiplication.
CCSS.Math.Content.2.OA.C.3 Determine whether a group of objects (up to 20) has an odd or even number of members, e.g., by pairing objects or counting them by 2s; write an equation to express an even number as a sum of two equal addends.

Represent and interpret data.
CCSS.Math.Content.2.MD.D.10 Draw a picture graph and a bar graph (with single-unit scale) to represent a data set with up to four categories. Solve simple put-together, take-apart, and compare problems using information presented in a bar graph.

Elementary:
Solve problems involving the four operations, and identify and explain patterns in arithmetic.
CCSS.Math.Content.3.OA.D.8 Solve two-step word problems using the four operations. Represent these problems using equations with a letter standing for the unknown quantity. Assess the reasonableness of answers using mental computation and estimation strategies including rounding.

CCSS.Math.Content.3.OA.D.9 Identify arithmetic patterns (including patterns in the addition table or multiplication table), and explain them using properties of operations. *For example, observe that 4 times a number is always even, and explain why 4 times a number can be decomposed into two equal addends.*

Develop understanding of fractions as numbers.
CCSS.Math.Content.3.NF.A.1 Understand a fraction $\frac{1}{b}$ as the quantity formed by 1 part when *a* whole is partitioned into *b* equal parts; understand a fraction $\frac{a}{b}$ as the quantity formed by *a* parts of size $\frac{1}{b}$.

Generate and analyze patterns.
CCSS.Math.Content.4.OA.C.5 Generate a number or shape pattern that follows a given rule. Identify apparent features of the pattern that were not explicit in the rule itself. *For example, given the rule "Add 3" and the starting number 1, generate terms in the resulting sequence and observe that the terms appear to alternate between odd and even numbers. Explain informally why the numbers will continue to alternate in this way.*

Analyze patterns and relationships.
CCSS.Math.Content.5.OA.B3 Generate two numerical patterns using two given rules. Identify apparent relationships between corresponding terms. Form ordered pairs consisting of corresponding terms from

the two patterns, and graph the ordered pairs on a coordinate plane. *For example, given the rule "Add 3" and the starting number 0, and given the rule "Add 6" and the starting number 0, generate terms in the resulting sequences, and observe that the terms in one sequence are twice the corresponding terms in the other sequence. Explain informally why this is so.*

Graph points on the coordinate plane to solve real-world and mathematical problems.

CCSS.Math.Content.5.G.A.2 Represent real-world and mathematical problems by graphing points in the first quadrant of the coordinate plane, and interpret coordinate values of points in the context of the situation.

(Common Core State Standards Initiative, 2012a)

Primary Example

A reproducible version of this tool is available in Appendix A (p. 148).

Guided Facilitation

What's My Move? initially provides children a game environment in which to develop familiarity with positional words while engaging in problem solving and critical thinking. The activity allows students the opportunity to specify their locations while beginning to understand the distinction between relative positions and absolute positions, such as north, south, east, or west or their home address. Revisiting the activity later provides opportunities to model, first with people and then with mathematical sentences. Questions can be asked in a more traditional format as well as with the unknown in various positions. Students can be asked to generate their own questions, especially as they progress from kindergarten through grades 1 and 2. A data table with four categories showing the same data set can be studied. This provides a context in which to look at sets that are "the same" or equal and opportunities to create sets with "one more" or "one less" than the set being studied. Patterns are discovered and discussed throughout the development of the activity.

This activity can be used throughout the year in the primary classroom to develop a variety of skills. Early in kindergarten you can give each child a game board and ask, "What do you see?" This will allow you to check the children's knowledge of colors, shapes, and basic positional words. Give children colored transparent counters to place on the child's face or circle, depending upon which board you are using. You can then begin a series of directions, such as "Move the blue counter to the space to the right around the corner of the table/rectangle" or "Jump the blue counter with the red counter around the corner of the table/rectangle."

Once the children have been able to follow the directions on their game board, choose a demonstration group of two students. Choosing one boy and one girl makes it easier to distinguish which players began on the each side and allows students to keep track of the direction the players are moving. Allow the children to work together to complete the activity. The class may provide hints for the players if they are having trouble.

> 💬 "Tommy, can you tell us where you are sitting in relation to Leslie?"

As the children are working, have them describe where they are with positional words—for example, "Tommy is across from Leslie," "Tommy just moved to his right," or "Leslie is moving to her left."

> 💬 "Class, how many slides did you see? How many jumps? How many moves were there altogether?"

Also, have children count the number of moves as they happen. One group can also count slides while one group counts jumps, and then they can total the moves and/or create a mathematical sentence representing the moves.

Once the two players have successfully completed the activity with three moves, have them repeat the activity while the rest of the class records the movements, looking for patterns. You can have part of the class record "boy" (B) versus "girl" (G) moves and the remaining part of the class record "slides" (S) versus "jumps" (J) to get the patterns below.

B G B   S J S

> 💬 "Boys and girls, what do you notice about this first pattern?" "What about the second pattern?"

Discuss what observations students have about the patterns they saw. Various answers include, but are not limited to the following:

> 💬 "How many slides were there?" "How many jumps?" "How many moves were there altogether?" "If there was only 1 jump, some slides, and 3 moves altogether, how many slides were there?"

1. It begins with a boy (B) and ends with a boy (B).
2. There is a total of 3 moves: 2 slides and 1 jump. Ask students to represent this with a mathematical sentence. You could also frame the question to reflect the unknown in a position other than the total.
3. The pattern is a palindrome. (Children love to hunt for palindromes, both numerical and verbal.)

● ● ● ● ● ● ● ● ● ● ● ● ● ● ● ● ● ●

A reproducible version of this tool is available in Appendix A (p. 151).

Now have the students repeat the activity with two boys sitting on one side and two girls sitting on the other side.

NOTE: It is necessary to differentiate between B_1, B_2, G_1, and G_2 for some of the questions below.

Once the group has successfully completed the activity with 8 moves, have them repeat the activity while the rest of the class records the movements, looking for patterns as before. Again you can have part of the class record "boy" (B) versus "girl" (G) moves and the remaining part of the class record "slides" (S) versus "jumps" (J) to get the patterns below. You will also want someone to record the moves for B_1, B_2, G_1, and G_2.

B G G B B G G B   S J S J J S J S

Discuss what observations students have about the patterns. Various answers include, but are not limited to the following:

> "Boys and girls, what do you notice about this first pattern?" "What about the second pattern?"

1. It begins with a boy (B) and ends with a boy (B). NOTE: The same would be true if the exercise had begun with a girl.

💬 "Was there an even or odd number of jumps? How do you know? Of slides? How do you know? When you combine the moves, is the total even or odd? Why do you think that is?"

💬 "How many slides were there?" "How many jumps?" "What numeral would I use?" "What number word?" "How many moves were there altogether?" "If there were some jumps, 3 slides, and 8 moves altogether, how many jumps were there?"

2. There seems to be a repeated pattern of BGGB and then BGGB.
3. After the initial move, there are consecutive team moves: B GG BB GG B.
4. There is a jump after the first slide, but 2 jumps after the second slide. But it is not a growing pattern.
5. There are 4 boy (B) moves and 4 girl (G) moves.
6. There is a total of 8 moves.
7. The pattern is a palindrome.

$$B_2 \quad G_2 \quad G_1 \quad B_2 \quad B_1 \quad G_2 \quad G_1 \quad B_1$$
$$S \quad J \quad S \quad J \quad J \quad S \quad J \quad S$$

Guide the children to create a table, bar graph, or pictograph with the data they collected about each individual player. In the data shown here, B_1 and G_1 are the players sitting next to the wall. This table includes four data sets that have equal numbers of pieces of data.

Number of Moves by Each Child			
4			
3			
2			
1			
B_1	B_2	G_1	G_2

The next step is to determine the number of moves by each player. Once the students have created their bar graphs (or pictographs), have them generate questions similar to the ones in the sidebar. They can then model their questions with equations.

It is important for students to understand the relationship between the equation and the physical movements from the exercise. This is the most important reason for doing the activity. Students need to understand that equations are developed in order to explain physical quantities and their relationship to one another. By using a real scenario and collecting actual data, students are better able to see the relationships and determine the mathematical connection.

> "How many moves did each player make?" "How many moves did the boys make altogether?" "How many moves did the girls make altogether?" "If boy 1 made 3 moves, girl 1 made 4 moves, and boy 1, girl 1, and girl 2 together made 9 moves, how many moves did girl 2 make?" "Model this with a math sentence." "How many more moves did boy 1 make than girl 2?"

NOTE: If students ask at this point why the game uses only an even number of people, ask them to hold that question. It will be addressed as an extension.

Key Vocabulary and Concept Development
- number
- quantity
- data
- bar graph/pictograph
- even
- odd
- palindrome
- equation
- unknown

Possible Extension Questions

1. If two tables make the same moves, how many slides and jumps will there be altogether?
2. If you have 2 slides and 1 jump, how many more slides do you have than jumps?
3. If you repeat this pattern three times, what would the seventh move be?
4. When one group of students completes this activity, you get an odd number of moves. When the second table does this, do you get an odd or even number of moves?
5. How could you use the boy-girl-boy pattern to model the commutative property?
6. Can this pattern with this setup be extended?
7. What happens if the number of people increased by one rather than two?
8. When you do this extension with three players and one open space, the pattern will be the following (given you have one girl and two boys; the pattern would be similar for one boy and two girls):

G_1	B_2	B_1	G_1	B_1
S	J	S	J	S

Elementary Example

A reproducible version of this tool is available in Appendix A (p. 151).

> **NOTE:** If this activity is being used in early third grade, refer to the primary Guided Facilitation (page 89) for foundational material.

Guided Facilitation

When used in the elementary grades, What's My Move? builds upon concepts developed in the primary grades. Patterns are discovered and discussed throughout the development of the activity. Initially the patterns are simple letter patterns, but can be developed through a table of values and then extended to modeling the pattern with a mathematical sentence. Two patterns can be discussed in relation to each other and then graphed in the Cartesian coordinate system.

Begin with a demonstration group of four students. Choosing two boys and two girls makes it easier to distinguish which players began on the same side and allows students to keep track of the direction the players are moving. Allow the players to work together to complete the activity. The class may provide hints for the players if they are having trouble.

Once the demonstration group has successfully completed the exercise with 8 moves, have the players repeat the activity while the rest of the class records the movements, looking for patterns. You can have part of the class record "boy" (B) versus "girl" (G) moves and the remaining part of the class record "slides" (S) versus "jumps" (J) to get the following patterns.

$$B_2 \quad G_2 \quad G_1 \quad B_2 \quad B_1 \quad G_2 \quad G_1 \quad B_1$$
$$S \quad J \quad S \quad J \quad J \quad S \quad J \quad S$$

NOTE: It is not necessary to differentiate between B_1, B_2, G_1, and G_2 since it will not affect the pattern being developed.

💬 "Was there an even or odd number of jumps? Of slides? When you combine the moves, is the total even or odd? Why do you think that is?" "Can you generalize a conjecture for combining even numbers or for combining odd numbers?"

Begin with the first pattern and discuss what observations students have about the pattern. Various answers include, but are not limited to the following:

1. The pattern begins with a boy (B) and ends with a boy (B).
   NOTE: The same would be true if the exercise began with a girl.
2. There seems to be a repeated pattern of BGGB and then BGGB.
3. After the initial move, there are consecutive team moves: B GG BB GG B.
4. There are 4 boy (B) moves and 4 girl (G) moves.
5. The pattern is a palindrome.

Continue the discussion by having students discuss the second pattern of slides (S) and jumps (J). Various answers include, but are not limited to the following:

💬 "Would the slide-jump pattern have been the same if we had started with a girl instead of a boy? Why or why not?"

1. The pattern begins with a slide (S) and ends with a slide (S).
2. There seems to be a reflexive pattern of SJSJ and then JSJS.
3. There are 4 slides (S) and 4 jumps (J).
4. The pattern is a palindrome.
5. There is a jump after the first slide, but 2 jumps after the second slide.

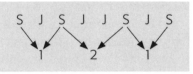

Let students know that these patterns may provide useful clues as the exercise continues.

Transition by asking students the sidebar questions.

Typically, students respond to the question on the right with such answers as 10 (adding 4 to the number of people), 12 (multiplying the number of people by 2), or 18 (multiplying the number of people by 3).

💬 "Given the patterns and knowing that with 4 people it took 8 moves, how many moves do you predict it would take for 6 people? Upon what criteria are you basing your answer?"

NOTE: If students ask at this point why the game uses only an even number of people, ask them to hold that question. It will be addressed as an extension exercise.

● ●

Now assign students to groups of six, ensuring there is some visual cue that distinguishes students on one side of the table from the other (boy-girl, glasses-no glasses, shirt colors, etc.). If there are no distinguishing characteristics, you can place colored sticky notes on students' shirts. Explain that students will check their predictions by completing the exercise with six people and recording the number of moves. *(The answer is 15 moves.)*

Ask students to repeat this exercise, but this time record the slide-jump sequence.

NOTE: The slide-jump pattern will be the focused pattern for the exercise. The boy-girl pattern can be used as an extension question.

You can use various methods, such as the following:

1. Complete the exercise physically with six people.
2. Use manipulatives, such as colored chips, to simulate the movements.
3. Continue the S-J pattern on paper and then count the number of moves.

💭 "How many moves would it take if there were 8 people?" "How did you think about that?"

Once finished, have students determine how many moves it would take with eight people and describe the method used for solving.

Guide students to develop a table and look for a numeric pattern; some students may recognize they could get additional data by doing the exercise with two people to get more data.

P = number of people
M = number of moves
S = number of slides
J = number of jumps

# of people (P)	# of moves (M)
4	8
6	15
8	?

+ 7

Many students incorrectly believe the answer is 22 because they assume it is constantly increasing by 7. Encourage them to use other methods or find additional data (without telling them to use two students—ask questions to allow them to realize this).

Once an answer of *24 moves* has been reached, ask students to individually consider the number of moves it would take for ten people. This will assess whether all students have recognized a pattern and are able to use the pattern for additional situations.

✏️ **NOTE:** At this point, students will typically notice that the number of moves is increasing by consecutive odd integers.

The same methods used for determining the number of moves for eight people can be continued; however, some are not conducive to arriving at the answer in an efficient and timely manner. For example, it is not feasible to physically arrange 100 people to complete the activity. The same could be said for using manipulatives. Completing the table by adding consecutive odd integers would take considerable time and space, as would the strategy of continuing with the S-J or B-G patterns.

However, aspects of these methods could be used to help students identify additional patterns. For example, students could expand the table to look for relationships between the types of movements. In the table on the next page, the following can be observed:

1. The number of people (P) = number of slides (S).

# of people (P)	# of slides (S)
4	4
6	6
8	8

2. The number of jumps (J) is a product of repeated multiplication, which leads to an extension in the discussion of a perfect square. *My Full Moon Is Square*, by Elinor J. Pinczes, is a revelant trade book that will help students visualize the concept of perfect squares.

# of people (P)	# of slides (S)	# of jumps (J)	# of moves (M)
4	4	$4 = 2 \cdot 2 = 2^2$	8
6	6	$9 = 3 \cdot 3 = 3^2$	15
8	8	$16 = 4 \cdot 4 = 4^2$	24

3. Students can conclude that the total number of moves is equivalent to the sum of the number of slides and the number of jumps.

# of moves = # of slides + # of jumps

# of people (P)	# of slides (S)	# of jumps (J)	# of moves (M)
4	4	$4 = 2 \cdot 2 = 2^2$	8
6	6	$9 = 3 \cdot 3 = 3^2$	15
8	8	$16 = 4 \cdot 4 = 4^2$	24

Questions such as these can be discussed:
- A group completed 63 moves and recorded 49 jumps. How many fewer slides were there than jumps? Show their thinking using an equation or model.
- How many people were in the group described above? How do you know?

4. Students can now see that the number of moves is increasing by consecutive odd numbers as the number of people increases constantly by two.

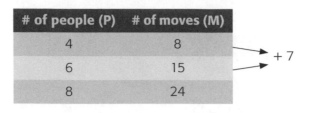

# of people (P)	# of moves (M)
4	8
6	15
8	24

# of moves for 6 people = # of moves for 4 people + 7
# of moves for 8 people = # of moves for 6 people + 9

Students could continue this pattern a few more times to check the conjecture and check it with a model.

Another pattern can be seen between the number of people and the number of moves. The 2.5 can be dealt with in terms of "two times" plus "half of" as a strategy. This pattern can also be easily extended to ten or more people.

# of people (P)		# of moves (M)
4	multiplied by 2 =	8
6	multiplied by 2.5 =	15
8	multiplied by 3 =	24

> "Does the number of people determine the number of moves or does the number of moves determine the number of people?"

5. Students can now graph the data on a coordinate grid.

Ask the students the questions in the sidebar. They should see that the number of people is what determines how many moves have to be made. The ordered pairs will have the number of people as the first element, the x-value, and the number of moves as the second element, the y-value.

> "How would you describe the patterns you used to develop the ordered pairs in connection with the plot of the ordered pairs?"

Guide students to label the horizontal axis "Number of People" and the vertical axis "Number of Moves." Then have them plot the points from the table. The graph should look something like the one on the next page. Ask students to talk about the graph and the points they plotted. Discuss the pattern used to generate the x-values and the y-values and how they differed.

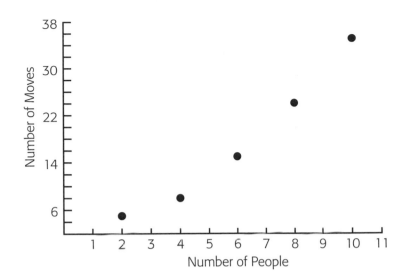

It is important for students to understand the relationship between the equation used to represent the data in the table and the physical movements from the exercise. This is the most important reason for doing the activity. Students need to understand that tables, graphs, and equations are developed in order to explain physical quantities and their relationship to one another. By using a real scenario and collecting actual data, students are better able to see the relationships and determine the mathematical connection.

Key Vocabulary and Concept Development

- data
- coordinate plane
- horizontal axis
- vertical axis
- even
- odd
- palindrome
- equation
- unknown
- perfect square

Possible Extension Questions

1. What happens if the number of people increased by one rather than two?
2. When you do this extension with three players and one open space, the pattern will be the following (given you have one girl and two boys; the pattern would be similar for one boy and two girls):

$$G_1 \ B_2 \ B_1 \ G_1 \ B_1$$
$$S \ \ J \ \ S \ \ J \ \ S$$

How does this pattern differ from the patterns collected with even numbers of people? How would the data table change?

3. How would using data collected from the boy-girl pattern be similar and/or different from the data gathered from the slide-jump pattern?

Possible Extension Activity

Students may be familiar with palindromes from their study of English. There are also many palindromes found in mathematics. Let students study palindromic numbers, palindromic money, and palindromic time and dates.

Appendix A

Five-Step Problem-Solving Process

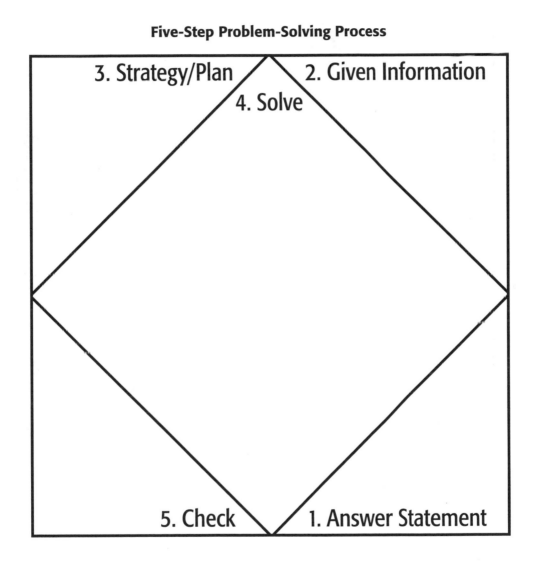

3. Strategy/Plan

2. Given Information

4. Solve

5. Check

1. Answer Statement

Five-Step Problem-Solving Process

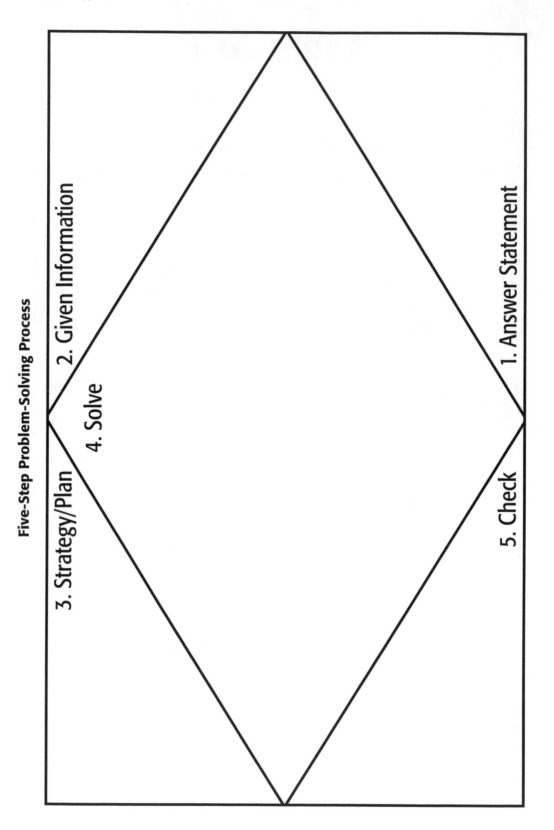

2. Given Information

1. Answer Statement

4. Solve

3. Strategy/Plan

5. Check

Visual Vocabulary Concept Mapping

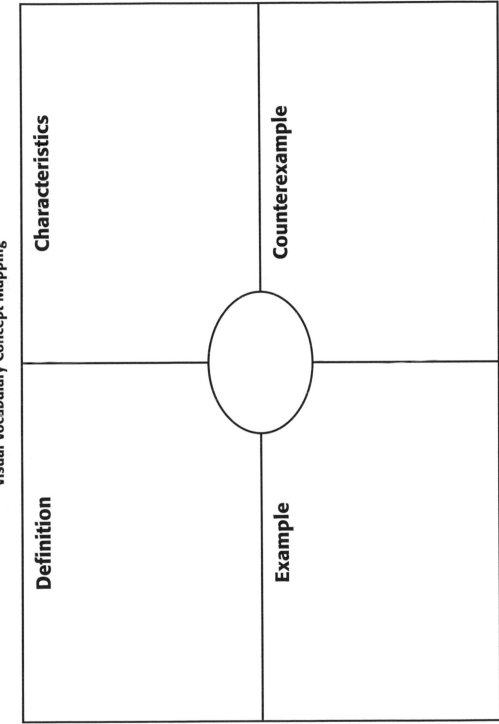

Characteristics

Counterexample

Definition

Example

Puzzling Problems: Primary

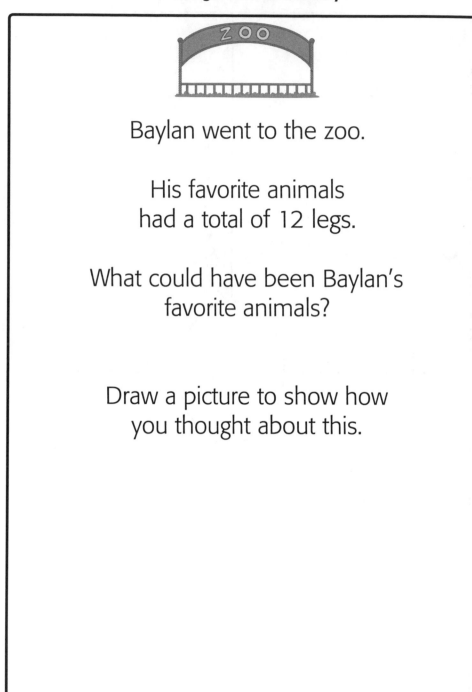

Baylan went to the zoo.

His favorite animals
had a total of 12 legs.

What could have been Baylan's
favorite animals?

Draw a picture to show how
you thought about this.

Think about Baylan's favorite animals you drew.

Are there other animals that could have been his favorites?

Draw a picture to show other animals that might have a total of 12 legs.

Write a math sentence to show
how you came up with 12 legs
for your first set of animals.

Write a math sentence to show
how you came up with 12 legs for
your second set of animals.

Puzzling Problems: Grades 2–3

Linda saw two types of butterflies in her grandmother's garden. One type had four spots on its wings. The second type had 5 spots on its wings.

If there were more than one of each type of butterfly in the garden, how many spots could Linda have seen in all?

List at least 10 numbers to show the total number of spots Linda might have seen.

Explain the strategy you used to arrive at the total number of spots possible.

Are there any numbers that could not represent the total number of spots she saw? Why or why not?

Puzzling Problems: Grades 4–5

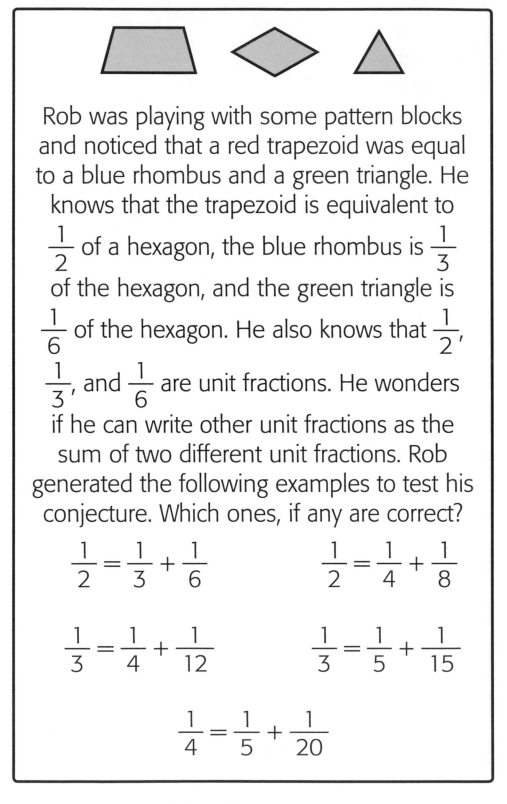

Rob was playing with some pattern blocks and noticed that a red trapezoid was equal to a blue rhombus and a green triangle. He knows that the trapezoid is equivalent to $\frac{1}{2}$ of a hexagon, the blue rhombus is $\frac{1}{3}$ of the hexagon, and the green triangle is $\frac{1}{6}$ of the hexagon. He also knows that $\frac{1}{2}$, $\frac{1}{3}$, and $\frac{1}{6}$ are unit fractions. He wonders if he can write other unit fractions as the sum of two different unit fractions. Rob generated the following examples to test his conjecture. Which ones, if any are correct?

$$\frac{1}{2} = \frac{1}{3} + \frac{1}{6} \qquad\qquad \frac{1}{2} = \frac{1}{4} + \frac{1}{8}$$

$$\frac{1}{3} = \frac{1}{4} + \frac{1}{12} \qquad\qquad \frac{1}{3} = \frac{1}{5} + \frac{1}{15}$$

$$\frac{1}{4} = \frac{1}{5} + \frac{1}{20}$$

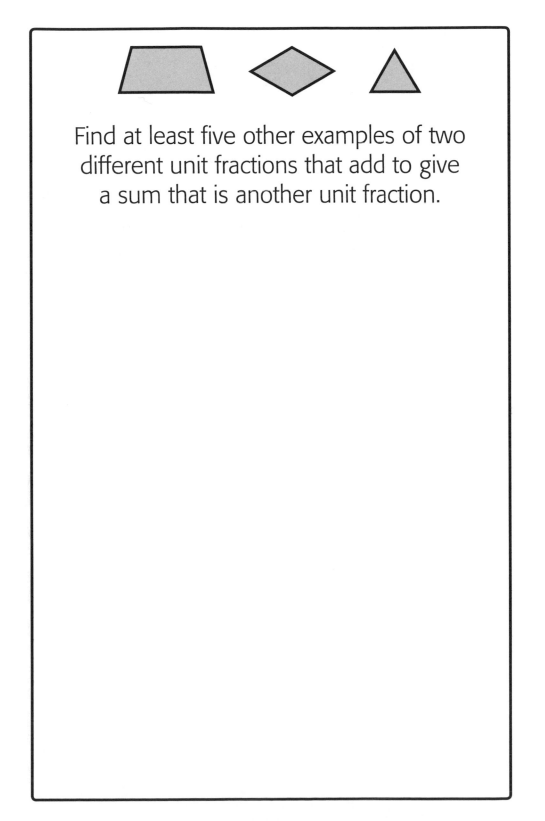

Find at least five other examples of two different unit fractions that add to give a sum that is another unit fraction.

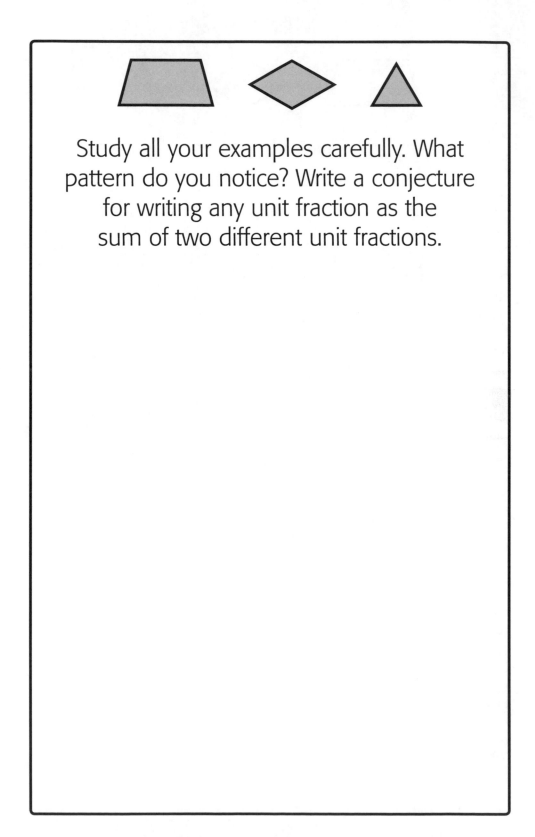

Study all your examples carefully. What pattern do you notice? Write a conjecture for writing any unit fraction as the sum of two different unit fractions.

Puzzling Problems Answer Keys

Grades K–1

For the first part of this problem, children may draw various animals. For example, they could draw an elephant with four legs, a lion with four legs, and a giraffe with four legs.

For the second part, a child might choose to use the elephant with four legs, an ostrich with two legs, a monkey with two legs (if they consider a monkey as having two legs and two arms), and a tiger with four legs.

For the third part, they need to represent their animals with correct numerical quantities. In the examples above, the mathematical equations would be $4 + 4 + 4 = 12$ and $4 + 2 + 2 + 4 = 12$.

Grades 2–3

The first part of this problem is very open-ended. There are many possible solutions. There could be one butterfly of each type so $4 + 5 = 9$, one four-spotted and two five-spotted butterflies so $4 + 5 + 5 = 14$, and so forth. This is a good opportunity for students to understand the benefit of constructing a table to record systematic values in order to begin to see patterns.

Total Spots on the Butterflies			
Number of four-spot butterflies	Number of five-spot butterflies		Total number of spots
1	1	4 + 5	9
1	2	4 + 5 + 5	14
1	3	4 + 5 + 5 + 5	19
. . .	. . .	. . .	. . .
2	1	4 + 4 + 5	13
2	2	4 + 4 + 5 + 5	18

For the second part of the problem, make sure the students connect a correct strategy to the totals they calculated. Students can use repeated addition or multiplication and addition for a more efficient way to approach the calculations.

The third part requires students to reason about their possible set of answers. The numbers 0–8 cannot be answers since there has to be at least one of each type of butterfly. Let students tinker with the problem and/or tables for a few days (this could become an interactive bulletin board–type problem) to see what other numbers might be impossible to have as totals—for example, 10, 11, and 12. The table below reveals a couple of patterns. As you increase the number of butterflies with four spots, you increase the total by 4 (going across the table). As you increase the number of five-spot butterflies, you increase the total by 5 (going down each column).

	Possible totals			
	1 four-spot	2 four-spots	3 four-spots	4 four-spots
1 five-spot	9	13	17	21
2 five-spots	14	18	22	26
3 five-spots	19	23	27	31
4 five-spots	24	28	32	36
5 five-spots	29	33	37	41

Grades 4–5

$$\frac{1}{2} = \frac{1}{3} + \frac{1}{6}$$

$$\frac{1}{3} = \frac{1}{4} + \frac{1}{12}$$

$$\frac{1}{4} = \frac{1}{5} + \frac{1}{20}$$

$$\frac{1}{2} = \frac{1}{4} + \frac{1}{8}$$

$$\frac{1}{3} = \frac{1}{5} + \frac{1}{15}$$

Only Rob's first, second, and third equations at the left are correct. The last two, using the 2, 4, and 8 as denominators and the 3, 5, and 15 as denominators, are incorrect.

Students can generate several other examples. (This is a good activity to use as the problem of the week or as an interactive bulletin board so students can work on it over a period of time.) A couple more examples are shown below.

$$\frac{1}{5} = \frac{1}{6} + \frac{1}{3} \qquad \frac{1}{6} = \frac{1}{7} + \frac{1}{42}$$

Students should have enough prior experiences with patterns to begin to see that one unit fraction needs to have a denominator that is one more than the unit fraction being decomposed. The second unit fraction has a denominator that is the product of the other two.

ABC Sum Race Sample Cards

A. Six buttons are in the basket. Two are yellow. The rest are pink. How many buttons are pink?

B. Leslie has three more stickers than Tammy. Tammy has seven stickers. How many stickers does Leslie have?

C. There are some orange slices on the plate. Baylan ate four orange slices. There is one slice remaining. How many orange slices were on the plate before?

A. How many more are in the right group than in the left group?

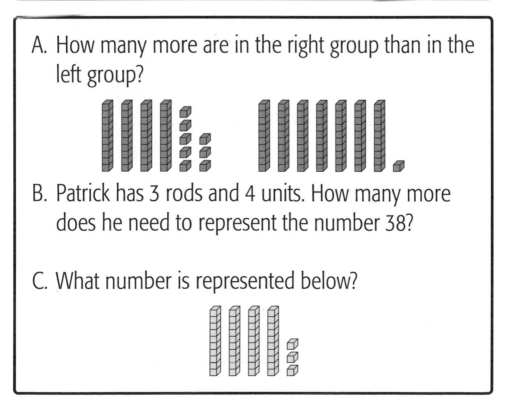

B. Patrick has 3 rods and 4 units. How many more does he need to represent the number 38?

C. What number is represented below?

A. $4 \times ? = 20$

B. $? \times 7 = 56$

C. $10 \times 22 = ?$

A. Alex is $2\frac{1}{2}$ years younger than his sister. His sister is 6 years old. How old is Alex?

B. Jamal ran some distance around the school's track. Patrick joins him for the run. They run another $1\frac{1}{4}$ laps around the track. Now Jamal has run $3\frac{1}{2}$ laps total. How many laps did he run before Patrick joined him?

C. A cookie recipe calls for $\frac{1}{3}$ of a cup of butter. Maya only has $\frac{1}{4}$ of a cup of butter. How much does she need to borrow from her neighbor so she can make cookies?

A. I am a 3-D figure called a cube. I have 6 faces. How many vertices do I have?

B. I am a regular, 6-sided, 2-D figure. How many lines of symmetry do I have?

C. I am a quadrilateral that is sometimes a square. What is the measure of one of my interior angles?

ABC Sum Race Scorecards

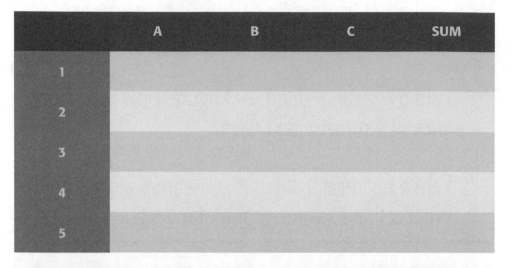

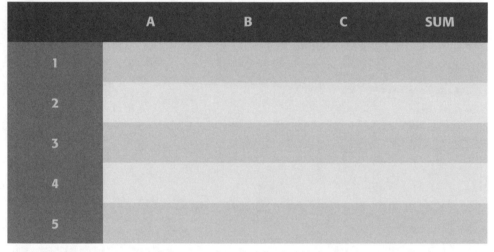

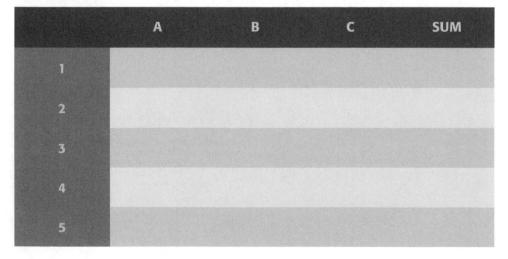

ABC Sum Race Answer Key

	A	B	C	SUM
1	4	10	5	19
2	23	4	43	70
3	5	8	220	233
4	$3\frac{1}{2}$	$2\frac{1}{4}$	$\frac{1}{12}$	$5\frac{5}{6}$
5	8	6	90	104

Scorecard

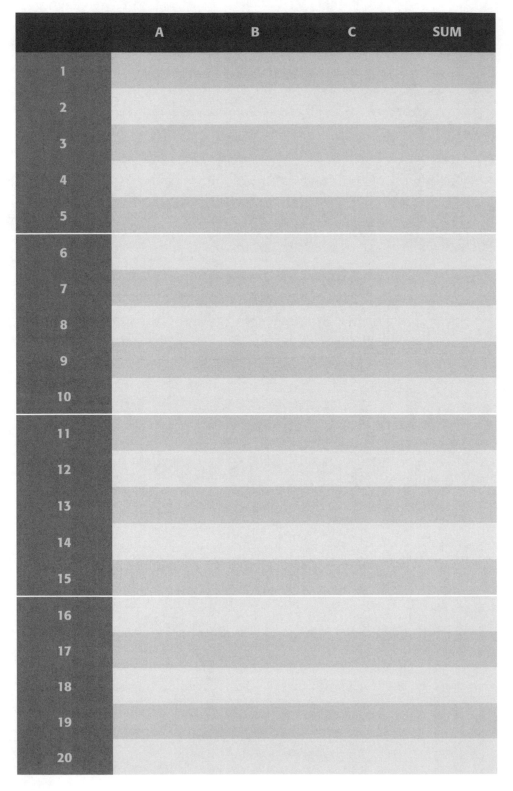

	A	B	C	SUM
1				
2				
3				
4				
5				
6				
7				
8				
9				
10				
11				
12				
13				
14				
15				
16				
17				
18				
19				
20				

Scorecard

	A	B	C	SUM
1				
2				
3				
4				
5				
6				
7				
8				
9				
10				
11				
12				
13				
14				
15				
16				
17				
18				
19				
20				

Grid Games: What's My Shape?

Correctly name each shape and identify as flat or solid.

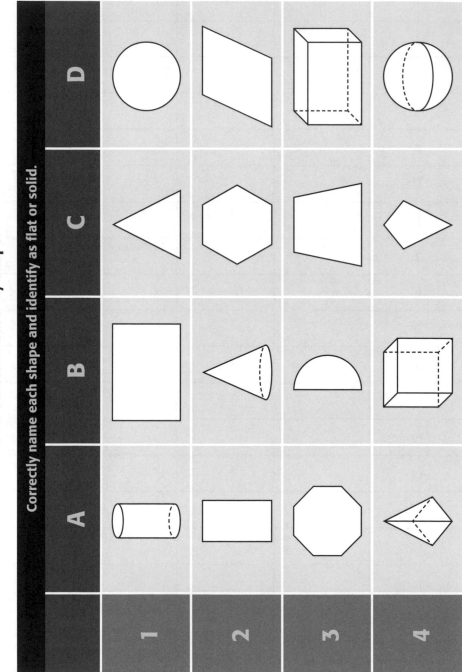

What's My Shape? Scorecard

	A	B	C	D
1				
2				
3				
4				

Grid Games Answer Keys

What's My Shape? Answer Key			
	A	**B**	**C**	**D**
1	cylinder	rectangle	triangle	circle
2	square	cone	hexagon	rhombus
3	octagon	semicircle	trapezoid	rectangular prism
4	pyramid	cube	kite	sphere

What's My Shape? Answer Key			
	A	**B**	**C**	**D**
1	solid	flat	flat	flat
2	flat	solid	flat	flat
3	flat	flat	flat	solid
4	solid	solid	flat	solid

Grid Games: Perimeter and Area

Find the perimeter and area of each figure below.

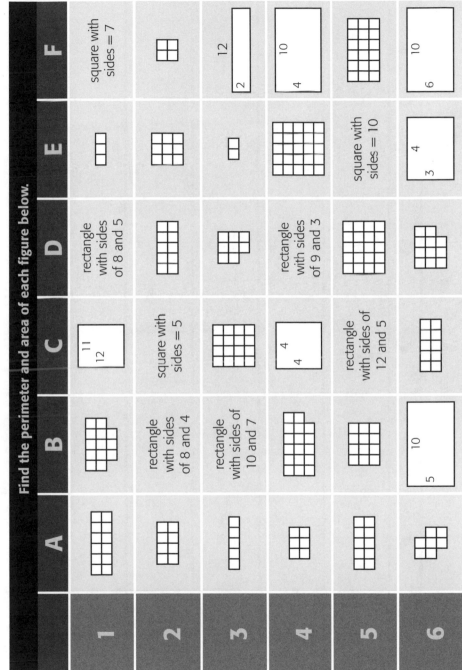

Perimeter and Area Scorecard

	A	B	C	D	E	F
1						
2						
3						
4						
5						
6						

Grid Games Answer Keys

Perimeter Answer Key						
	A	B	C	D	E	F
1	16	16	46	26	8	28
2	12	24	20	14	12	8
3	12	34	16	12	6	28
4	10	18	16	24	20	28
5	14	14	34	18	40	18
6	12	30	14	14	14	32

Area Answer Key						
	A	B	C	D	E	F
1	12	13	132	40	3	49
2	8	32	25	10	9	4
3	5	70	16	8	2	24
4	6	16	16	27	25	40
5	10	12	60	20	100	18
6	7	50	10	11	12	60

Matching Mania: One-Digit Operations

1 9 5	**2** 6 1
3 8 3	**4** 5 1
5 7 6	**6** 9 9
7 9 7	**8** 2 1
9 5 4	**10** 8 4
11 6 2	**12** 3 1
13 9 8	**14** 9 6
15 6 2	**16** 3 2
17 8 1	**18** 7 5

A. sum = 3	**R.** sum = 4
B. sum = 5	**Q.** sum = 6
C. sum = 7	**P.** sum = 9
D. sum = 8	**P.** sum = 9
D. sum = 8	**N.** sum = 11
F. sum = 13	**M.** sum = 12
G. sum = 14	**M.** sum = 12
H. sum = 15	**K.** sum = 16
I. sum = 17	**J.** sum = 18

a. **difference = 0**	**g.** **difference = 7**
b. **difference = 1**	**f.** **difference = 5**
b. **difference = 1**	**f.** **difference = 5**
b. **difference = 1**	**e.** **difference = 4**
b. **difference = 1**	**e.** **difference = 4**
b. **difference = 1**	**e.** **difference = 4**
c. **difference = 2**	**e.** **difference = 4**
c. **difference = 2**	**e.** **difference = 4**
c. **difference = 2**	**d.** **difference = 3**

One-Digit Operations Scorecards

Numbers	Sum	Difference
1		
2		
3		
4		
5		
6		
7		
8		
9		
10		
11		
12		
13		
14		
15		
16		
17		
18		

Numbers	Sum	Difference
1		
2		
3		
4		
5		
6		
7		
8		
9		
10		
11		
12		
13		
14		
15		
16		
17		
18		

One-Digit Operations Answer Key

Numbers	Sum	Difference
1	G	e
2	C	f
3	N	f
4	Q	e
5	F	b
6	J	a
7	K	c
8	A	b
9	P	b
10	M	e
11	D	e
12	R	c
13	I	b
14	H	d
15	D	e
16	B	b
17	P	g
18	M	c

Matching Mania: Factors and Primes

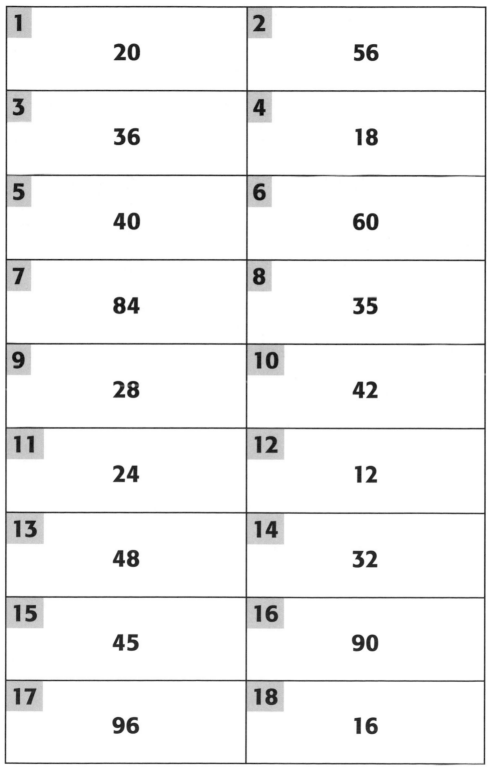

1 20	**2** 56
3 36	**4** 18
5 40	**6** 60
7 84	**8** 35
9 28	**10** 42
11 24	**12** 12
13 48	**14** 32
15 45	**16** 90
17 96	**18** 16

A. 1, 2, 3, 4, 6, 12	**R.** 1, 5, 7, 35
B. 1, 2, 3, 4, 6, 8, 12, 24, 48	**Q.** 1, 2, 3, 4, 6, 8, 12, 24
C. 1, 2, 4, 7, 14, 28	**P.** 1, 2, 4, 5, 8, 10, 20, 40
D. 1, 2, 4, 8, 16	**O.** 1, 2, 3, 6, 7, 14, 21, 42
E. 1, 2, 3, 4, 6, 7, 12, 14, 21, 28, 42, 84	**N.** 1, 3, 5, 9, 15, 45
F. 1, 2, 4, 8, 16, 32	**M.** 1, 2, 3, 4, 6, 9, 12, 18, 36
G. 1, 2, 3, 4, 6, 8, 12, 16, 24, 32, 48, 96	**L.** 1, 2, 3, 5, 6, 9, 10, 15, 18, 30, 45, 90
H. 1, 2, 4, 5, 10, 20	**K.** 1, 2, 4, 7, 8, 14, 28, 56
I. 1, 2, 3, 6, 9, 18	**J.** 1, 2, 3, 4, 6, 10, 15, 20, 30, 60

a. $2 \times 2 \times 2 \times 7$	**r.** $2 \times 2 \times 3$
b. $2 \times 2 \times 3 \times 3$	**q.** $2 \times 2 \times 2 \times 2 \times 3$
c. $2 \times 2 \times 2 \times 3$	**p.** $2 \times 2 \times 5$
d. $3 \times 3 \times 5$	**o.** $2 \times 2 \times 2 \times 2 \times 2$
e. $2 \times 2 \times 3 \times 5$	**n.** $2 \times 2 \times 2 \times 2$
f. $3 \times 3 \times 2$	**m.** $2 \times 2 \times 3 \times 7$
g. 5×7	**l.** $3 \times 3 \times 2 \times 5$
h. $2 \times 2 \times 7$	**k.** $2 \times 2 \times 2 \times 2 \times 2 \times 3$
i. $2 \times 3 \times 7$	**j.** $2 \times 2 \times 2 \times 5$

Factors and Primes Scorecards

Numbers	Factors	Prime Factors	Numbers	Factors	Prime Factors
1			1		
2			2		
3			3		
4			4		
5			5		
6			6		
7			7		
8			8		
9			9		
10			10		
11			11		
12			12		
13			13		
14			14		
15			15		
16			16		
17			17		
18			18		

Factors and Primes Answer Key

Numbers	Sum	Difference
1	H	p
2	K	a
3	M	b
4	I	f
5	P	j
6	J	e
7	E	m
8	R	g
9	C	h
10	O	i
11	Q	c
12	A	r
13	B	q
14	F	o
15	N	d
16	L	l
17	G	k
18	D	n

Matching Mania: Operations with Fractions 2

1 $3\dfrac{1}{2}$ $\quad$ $1\dfrac{3}{8}$	**2** $\dfrac{8}{9}$ $\quad$ $\dfrac{1}{3}$
3 $2\dfrac{1}{8}$ $\quad$ $\dfrac{2}{3}$	**4** $\dfrac{2}{3}$ $\quad$ $\dfrac{1}{6}$
5 $\dfrac{1}{2}$ $\quad$ $\dfrac{3}{8}$	**6** $2\dfrac{1}{6}$ $\quad$ $\dfrac{1}{3}$
7 $\dfrac{4}{5}$ $\quad$ $\dfrac{1}{4}$	**8** $3\dfrac{1}{2}$ $\quad$ $2\dfrac{1}{8}$
9 $3\dfrac{5}{6}$ $\quad$ $1\dfrac{1}{3}$	**10** $\dfrac{7}{8}$ $\quad$ $\dfrac{1}{3}$
11 $\dfrac{5}{6}$ $\quad$ $\dfrac{2}{3}$	**12** $3\dfrac{4}{5}$ $\quad$ $2\dfrac{2}{3}$
13 $4\dfrac{3}{5}$ $\quad$ $2\dfrac{2}{3}$	**14** $\dfrac{4}{5}$ $\quad$ $\dfrac{2}{3}$
15 $4\dfrac{3}{5}$ $\quad$ $3\dfrac{1}{4}$	**16** $3\dfrac{1}{5}$ $\quad$ $1\dfrac{3}{4}$

A. Sum $= 7\frac{17}{20}$	**R.** Sum $= 5\frac{1}{6}$
B. Sum $= 4\frac{19}{20}$	**Q.** Sum $= 1\frac{1}{20}$
C. Sum $= \frac{7}{8}$	**P.** Sum $= 2\frac{5}{6}$
D. Sum $= \frac{5}{6}$	**O.** Sum $= 1\frac{2}{9}$
E. Sum $= 6\frac{7}{15}$	**N.** Sum $= 2\frac{19}{24}$
F. Sum $= 5\frac{5}{8}$	**M.** Sum $= 7\frac{4}{15}$
G. Sum $= 4\frac{7}{8}$	**L.** Sum $= 1\frac{5}{24}$
H. Sum $= 1\frac{1}{2}$	**K.** Sum $= 1\frac{7}{15}$

A. **Difference** $= 2\frac{1}{8}$	**R.** **Difference** $= 1\frac{14}{15}$
B. **Difference** $= \frac{1}{2}$	**Q.** **Difference** $= 2\frac{1}{2}$
C. **Difference** $= \frac{5}{9}$	**P.** **Difference** $= 1\frac{1}{2}$
D. **Difference** $= \frac{1}{8}$	**O.** **Difference** $= 1\frac{11}{24}$
E. **Difference** $= \frac{13}{24}$	**N.** **Difference** $= 1\frac{3}{8}$
F. **Difference** $= \frac{2}{15}$	**M.** **Difference** $= \frac{11}{20}$
G. **Difference** $= \frac{1}{6}$	**L.** **Difference** $= 1\frac{9}{20}$
H. **Difference** $= 1\frac{2}{15}$	**K.** **Difference** $= 1\frac{7}{20}$

a. Product = $\dfrac{1}{9}$	**p.** Product = $5\dfrac{1}{9}$
b. Product = $1\dfrac{5}{12}$	**o.** Product = $\dfrac{8}{27}$
c. Product = $1\dfrac{4}{9}$	**n.** Product = $12\dfrac{4}{15}$
d. Product = $\dfrac{5}{9}$	**m.** Product = $\dfrac{3}{16}$
e. Product = $10\dfrac{2}{15}$	**l.** Product = $\dfrac{7}{24}$
f. Product = $\dfrac{1}{5}$	**k.** Product = $7\dfrac{7}{16}$
g. Product = $14\dfrac{19}{20}$	**j.** Product = $\dfrac{8}{15}$
h. Product = $5\dfrac{3}{5}$	**i.** Product = $4\dfrac{13}{16}$

a. Quotient $= 1\frac{1}{3}$	**p.** Quotient $= 1\frac{1}{4}$
b. Quotient $= 2\frac{7}{8}$	**o.** Quotient $= 3\frac{1}{4}$
c. Quotient $= 1\frac{29}{35}$	**n.** Quotient $= 3\frac{3}{16}$
d. Quotient $= 2\frac{6}{11}$	**m.** Quotient $= 2\frac{2}{3}$
e. Quotient $= 4$	**l.** Quotient $= 1\frac{1}{5}$
f. Quotient $= 1\frac{29}{40}$	**k.** Quotient $= 1\frac{11}{17}$
g. Quotient $= 2\frac{5}{8}$	**j.** Quotient $= 3\frac{1}{5}$
h. Quotient $= 1\frac{17}{40}$	**i.** Quotient $= 1\frac{27}{65}$

b. LCD = 6	**g.** LCD = 24
b. LCD = 6	**g.** LCD = 24
b. LCD = 6	**f.** LCD = 20
b. LCD = 6	**f.** LCD = 20
c. LCD = 8	**f.** LCD = 20
c. LCD = 8	**e.** LCD = 15
c. LCD = 8	**e.** LCD = 15
d. LCD = 9	**e.** LCD = 15

Operations with Fractions 2 Scorecards

Fractions	Sum	Difference	Product	Quotient	LCD
1					
2					
3					
4					
5					
6					
7					
8					
9					
10					
11					
12					
13					
14					
15					
16					

Fractions	Sum	Difference	Product	Quotient	LCD
1					
2					
3					
4					
5					
6					
7					
8					
9					
10					
11					
12					
13					
14					
15					
16					

Operations with Fractions 2 Answer Key

Fractions	Sum	Difference	Product	Quotient	LCD
1	G	A	i	d	c
2	O	C	o	m	d
3	N	O	b	n	g
4	D	B	a	e	b
5	C	D	m	a	c
6	P	P	c	o	b
7	Q	M	f	j	f
8	F	N	k	k	c
9	R	Q	p	b	b
10	L	E	l	g	g
11	H	G	d	p	b
12	E	H	e	h	e
13	M	R	n	f	e
14	K	F	j	l	e
15	A	K	g	i	f
16	B	L	h	c	f

www.gridgamesgalore.com

What's My Move?

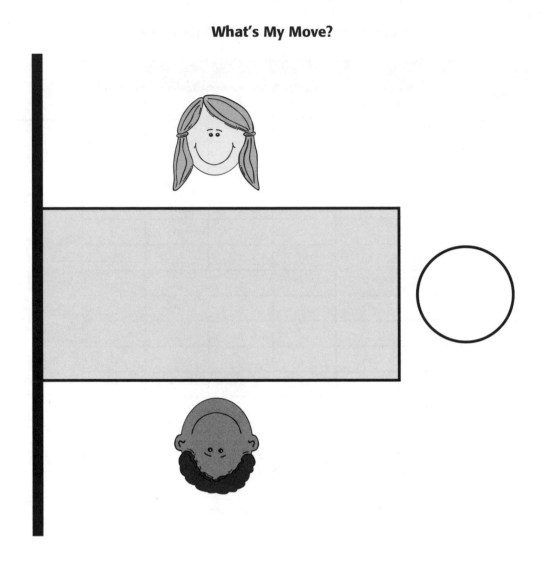

What's My Move?

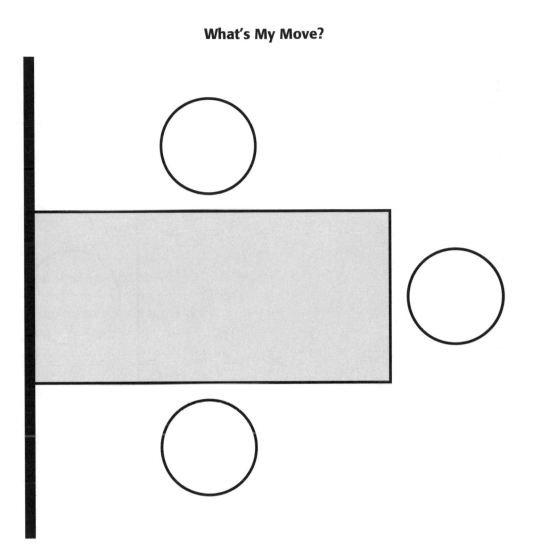

What's My Move?

What's My Move?

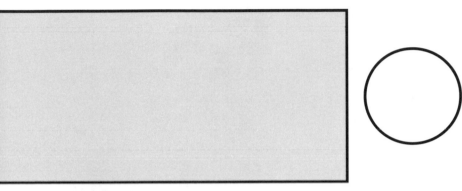

Appendix B

Standards for Mathematical Practice*

The Standards for Mathematical Practice describe varieties of expertise that mathematics educators at all levels should seek to develop in their students. These practices rest on important "processes and proficiencies" with longstanding importance in mathematics education. The first of these are the NCTM process standards of problem solving, reasoning and proof, communication, representation, and connections. The second are the strands of mathematical proficiency specified in the National Research Council's report *Adding It Up*: adaptive reasoning, strategic competence, conceptual understanding (comprehension of mathematical concepts, operations and relations), procedural fluency (skill in carrying out procedures flexibly, accurately, efficiently and appropriately), and productive disposition (habitual inclination to see mathematics as sensible, useful, and worthwhile, coupled with a belief in diligence and one's own efficacy).

1 Make sense of problems and persevere in solving them.

Mathematically proficient students start by explaining to themselves the meaning of a problem and looking for entry points to its solution. They analyze givens, constraints, relationships, and goals. They make conjectures about the form and meaning of the solution and plan a solution pathway rather than simply jumping into a solution attempt. They consider analogous problems, and try special cases and simpler forms of the original problem in order to gain insight into its solution. They monitor and evaluate their progress and change course if necessary. Older students might, depending on the context of the problem, transform algebraic expressions or change the viewing window on their graphing calculator to get the information they need. Mathematically proficient students can explain correspondences between equations, verbal descriptions, tables, and graphs or draw diagrams of important features and relationships, graph data, and search for regularity or trends. Younger students might rely on using

*Common Core State Standards Initiative. (2012). Standards for Mathematical Practice (pp. 6–8). Retrieved from http://www.corestandards.org/assets/CCSSI_Math%20Standards.pdf

concrete objects or pictures to help conceptualize and solve a problem. Mathematically proficient students check their answers to problems using a different method, and they continually ask themselves, "Does this make sense?" They can understand the approaches of others to solving complex problems and identify correspondences between different approaches.

2 Reason abstractly and quantitatively.

Mathematically proficient students make sense of quantities and their relationships in problem situations. They bring two complementary abilities to bear on problems involving quantitative relationships: the ability to *decontextualize*—to abstract a given situation and represent it symbolically and manipulate the representing symbols as if they have a life of their own, without necessarily attending to their referents—and the ability to *contextualize*, to pause as needed during the manipulation process in order to probe into the referents for the symbols involved. Quantitative reasoning entails habits of creating a coherent representation of the problem at hand; considering the units involved; attending to the meaning of quantities, not just how to compute them; and knowing and flexibly using different properties of operations and objects.

3 Construct viable arguments and critique the reasoning of others.

Mathematically proficient students understand and use stated assumptions, definitions, and previously established results in constructing arguments. They make conjectures and build a logical progression of statements to explore the truth of their conjectures. They are able to analyze situations by breaking them into cases, and can recognize and use counterexamples. They justify their conclusions, communicate them to others, and respond to the arguments of others. They reason inductively about data, making plausible arguments that take into account the context from which the data arose. Mathematically proficient students are also able to compare the effectiveness of two plausible arguments, distinguish correct logic or reasoning from that which is flawed, and—if there is a flaw in an argument— explain what it is. Elementary students can construct arguments using concrete referents such as objects, drawings, diagrams, and actions. Such arguments can make sense and be correct, even though they are not generalized or made formal until later grades. Later, students learn to determine domains to which an argument applies. Students at all grades can listen or read the arguments of others, decide whether they make sense, and ask useful questions to clarify or improve the arguments.

4 Model with mathematics.

Mathematically proficient students can apply the mathematics they know to solve problems arising in everyday life, society, and the workplace.

In early grades, this might be as simple as writing an addition equation to describe a situation. In middle grades, a student might apply proportional reasoning to plan a school event or analyze a problem in the community. By high school, a student might use geometry to solve a design problem or use a function to describe how one quantity of interest depends on another. Mathematically proficient students who can apply what they know are comfortable making assumptions and approximations to simplify a complicated situation, realizing that these may need revision later. They are able to identify important quantities in a practical situation and map their relationships using such tools as diagrams, two-way tables, graphs, flowcharts and formulas. They can analyze those relationships mathematically to draw conclusions. They routinely interpret their mathematical results in the context of the situation and reflect on whether the results make sense, possibly improving the model if it has not served its purpose.

5 Use appropriate tools strategically.

Mathematically proficient students consider the available tools when solving a mathematical problem. These tools might include pencil and paper, concrete models, a ruler, a protractor, a calculator, a spreadsheet, a computer algebra system, a statistical package, or dynamic geometry software. Proficient students are sufficiently familiar with tools appropriate for their grade or course to make sound decisions about when each of these tools might be helpful, recognizing both the insight to be gained and their limitations. For example, mathematically proficient high school students analyze graphs of functions and solutions generated using a graphing calculator. They detect possible errors by strategically using estimation and other mathematical knowledge. When making mathematical models, they know that technology can enable them to visualize the results of varying assumptions, explore consequences, and compare predictions with data. Mathematically proficient students at various grade levels are able to identify relevant external mathematical resources, such as digital content located on a website, and use them to pose or solve problems. They are able to use technological tools to explore and deepen their understanding of concepts.

6 Attend to precision.

Mathematically proficient students try to communicate precisely to others. They try to use clear definitions in discussion with others and in their own reasoning. They state the meaning of the symbols they choose, including using the equal sign consistently and appropriately. They are careful about specifying units of measure, and labeling axes to clarify the correspondence with quantities in a problem. They calculate accurately and efficiently, express numerical answers with a degree of precision appropriate for the problem context. In the elementary grades, students give carefully formulated explanations to each other. By the time they reach high school they have learned to examine claims and make explicit use of definitions.

7 Look for and make use of structure.

Mathematically proficient students look closely to discern a pattern or structure. Young students, for example, might notice that three and seven more is the same amount as seven and three more, or they may sort a collection of shapes according to how many sides the shapes have. Later, students will see 7×8 equals the well remembered $7 \times 5 + 7 \times 3$, in preparation for learning about the distributive property. In the expression $x^2 + 9x + 14$, older students can see the 14 as 2×7 and the 9 as $2 + 7$. They recognize the significance of an existing line in a geometric figure and can use the strategy of drawing an auxiliary line for solving problems. They also can step back for an overview and shift perspective. They can see complicated things, such as some algebraic expressions, as single objects or as being composed of several objects. For example, they can see $5 - 3(x - y)^2$ as 5 minus a positive number times a square and use that to realize that its value cannot be more than 5 for any real numbers x and y.

8 Look for and express regularity in repeated reasoning.

Mathematically proficient students notice if calculations are repeated, and look both for general methods and for shortcuts. Upper elementary students might notice when dividing 25 by 11 that they are repeating the same calculations over and over again, and conclude they have a repeating decimal. By paying attention to the calculation of slope as they repeatedly check whether points are on the line through (1, 2) with slope 3, middle school students might abstract the equation $(y - 2)/(x - 1) = 3$. Noticing the regularity in the way terms cancel when expanding $(x - 1)(x + 1)$, $(x - 1)(x^2 + x + 1)$, and $(x - 1)(x^3 + x^2 + x + 1)$ might lead them to the general formula for the sum of a geometric series. As they work to solve a problem, mathematically proficient students maintain oversight of the process, while attending to the details. They continually evaluate the reasonableness of their intermediate results.

Connecting the Standards for Mathematical Practice to the Standards for Mathematical Content

The Standards for Mathematical Practice describe ways in which developing student practitioners of the discipline of mathematics increasingly ought to engage with the subject matter as they grow in mathematical maturity and expertise throughout the elementary, middle and high school years. Designers of curricula, assessments, and professional development should all attend to the need to connect the mathematical practices to mathematical content in mathematics instruction.

The Standards for Mathematical Content are a balanced combination of procedure and understanding. Expectations that begin with the word "understand" are often especially good opportunities to connect the practices to the content. Students who lack understanding of a topic may rely on procedures too heavily. Without a flexible base from which to work, they may be less likely to consider analogous problems, represent problems coherently, justify conclusions, apply the mathematics to practical situations, use technology mindfully to work with the mathematics, explain the mathematics accurately to other students, step back for an overview, or deviate from a known procedure to find a shortcut. In short, a lack of understanding effectively prevents a student from engaging in the mathematical practices.

In this respect, those content standards which set an expectation of understanding are potential "points of intersection" between the Standards for Mathematical Content and the Standards for Mathematical Practice. These points of intersection are intended to be weighted toward central and generative concepts in the school mathematics curriculum that most merit the time, resources, innovative energies, and focus necessary to qualitatively improve the curriculum, instruction, assessment, professional development, and student achievement in mathematics.

Common Core State Standards for Mathematics K–5 Nomenclature Key

———◼———

Grade Level Identifiers	
Kindergarten	K
First Grade	1
Second Grade	2
Third Grade	3
Fourth Grade	4
Fifth Grade	5

Domain Identifiers		
Counting & Cardinality	CC	Kindergarten only
Operations & Algebraic Thinking	OA	Grades K, 1, 2, 3, 4, 5
Number & Operations in Base Ten	NBT	Grades K, 1, 2, 3, 4, 5
Measurement & Data	MD	Grades K, 1, 2, 3, 4, 5
Geometry	G	Grades K, 1, 2, 3, 4, 5
Number & Operations—Fractions	NF	Grades 3, 4, 5

CCSS.Math.Content.K.CC.A.1 is interpreted as the first standard in the first cluster in the Counting and Cardinality domain in the kindergarten standards.

Standards Alignment–Primary

Remember: The strategies can be used with any content standard. The list below simply references the ones used as examples.

	Counting and Cardinality (Kindergarten Only)	Operations and Algebraic Thinking	Number and Operations in Base Ten	Measurement and Data	Geometry
Problem-Solving Process				K.MD.A.1 K.MD.A.2 1.MD.A.1 1.MD.A.2 2.MD.B.5 2.MD.B.6	
Visual Vocabulary					K.G.A.2 1.G.A.3 2.G.A.3
Puzzling Problems		K.OA.A.1 K.OA.A.2 1.OA.A.1 1.OA.A.2 2.OA.B.2 2.OA.C.4			
ABC Sum Race	K.OA.A.2 1.OA.A.1		1.NBT.B.2 1.NBT.B.2a 1.NBT.B.2b 1.NBT.B.2c 1.NBT.3.3 1.NBT.C.4 2.NBT.B.5		

	Counting and Cardinality (Kindergarten Only)	Operations and Algebraic Thinking	Number and Operations in Base Ten	Measurement and Data	Geometry
Grid Games					K.G.A.2 K.G.A.3 1.G.A.1 2.G.A.1
Matching Mania		K.OA.A.5 1.OA.C.6 2.OA.B.2			
Walk This Way	K.CC.A.1 K.CC.A.2	K.OA.A.1 K.OA.A.2 K.OA.A.3 K.OA.A.4 K.OA.A.5 1.OA.A.1 1.OA.A.2 1.OA.B.3 1.OA.B.4 2.OA.A.1 2.OA.C.3		2.MD.B.6	
What's My Move?	K.CC.B.4 K.CC.B.4a K.CC.B.4b K.CC.B.4c K.CC.B.5	1.OA.A.1 1.OA.A.2 2.OA.A.1 2.OA.C.3	1.NBT.A.1	1.MD.C.4 2.MD.D.10	K.G.A.1

Standards Alignment–Elementary

Remember: The strategies can be used with any content standard. The list below simply references the ones used as examples.

	Operations and Algebraic Thinking	Number and Operations in Base Ten	Number and Operations—Fractions	Measurement and Data	Geometry
Problem-Solving Process				3.MD.C.7.b 3.MD.D.8 4.MD.A.3	
Visual Vocabulary			3.NF.A.1		3.G.A.2
Puzzling Problems	3.OA.A.1 3.OA.A.3		4.NF.B.3 4.NF.B.3a 5.NF.A.1		
ABC Sum Race	3.OA.A.4		4.NF.B.3 4.NF.B.3d 5.NF.A.2		3.G.A.1 4.G.A.3 5.G.B.3 5.G.B.4

	Operations and Algebraic Thinking	Number and Operations in Base Ten	Number and Operations—Fractions	Measurement and Data	Geometry
Grid Games				3.MD.C.6 3.MD.C.7 3.MD.C.7a 3.MD.C.7b 3.MD.C.7c 3.MD.C.7d 4.MD.A.3 5.MD.C.5 5.MD.C.5a	
Matching Mania	3.OA.B.6 4.OA.B.4 5.OA.B3	5.NBT.B6	5.NF.A.1 5.NF.B.6 5.NF.B.7		
Walk This Way	3.OA.D.9		4.NF.A.1 4.NF.A.2 4.NF.C.6 4.NF.C.7	3.MD.B.4	5.G.A.1 5.G.A.2
What's My Move?	3.OA.D.8 3.OA.D.9 4.OA.C.5 5.OA.B3		3.NF.A.1		5.G.A.2

References

Common Core State Standards Initiative. (2012a). *Common core state standards for mathematics.* Retrieved from http://www.corestandards.org/Math

Common Core State Standards Initiative. (2012b). *Standards for mathematical practice* (pp. 6–8). Retrieved from http://www.corestandards.org/assets/CCSSI_Math%20Standards.pdf

National Council of Teachers of Mathematics. (2005). *Principles and standards for school mathematics.* Reston, VA: NCTM.

Partnership for Assessment of Readiness for College and Careers (PARCC). (n.d.). *Connections to the PARCC assessment.* Retrieved from http://www.parcconline.org/mcf/mathematics/connections-parcc-assessment#_ftn1